spdr

srthM

dcyre

*spdri srthN dcyre**

JOE M. PULLIS, Ed.D.

Professor, Department of Office Administration
and Business Communication
College of Administration and Business
Louisiana Tech University

Glencoe Publishing Company
Mission Hills, California

***SPEEDWRITING
SHORTHAND
DICTIONARY
(abridged)**

Cheryl D. Pullis, M. Ed.
System Consultant

Calligraphy: Juana Silcox
Cover and interior design: Harkavy Publishing Services/Levavi & Levavi
System editor: Karl C. Illg, Jr.
Typesetter: Compolith Graphics
Printer: R. R. Donnelley

Copyright © 1984, 1977 by The Bobbs-Merrill Co., Inc.
Copyright © 1975, 1973, 1966, 1964, 1954, 1951, 1950, 1925 by Speedwriting Publishing
Company, Inc.

Copyrights transferred to Glencoe Publishing Company, a division of Macmillan, Inc.

Send all inquiries to:
Glencoe Publishing Company
15319 Chatsworth Street
Mission Hills, California 91345

Printed in the United States of America

Library of Congress Cataloging in Publication Data

Pullis, Joe M.

    Spdri srthN dcjre = Speedwriting shorthand dictionary (abridged)
    1. Shorthand—Speedwriting—Dictionaries.   I. Title.   II. Title: Speedwriting shorthand
dictionary (abridged)
Z56.2.S6A3 1984   653'.2'0321   83-22517

ISBN 0-02-685151-2
    2 3 4 5 6 7   90 89 88

CONTENTS

WORD DIVISION RULES

The *Speedwriting Shorthand Abridged Dictionary, Regency System*, contains shorthand outlines for over 6,000 of the most frequently used words in business communications, and all places where these words can correctly be divided in typewriting transcription applications are shown. The rules utilized for these word divisions are as follows.

1. Divide words only between syllables: dis·play, con·scious
   Thus, one-syllable words cannot be divided: strength, through

2. Do not divide a word of five or fewer letters: ideas, refer

3. Do not divide a proper noun, a contraction, an abbreviation, or a figure: America, shouldn't, A.S.P.C.A., $10,234.75

4. Do not divide a one- or two-letter syllable at the end of a word: ready, lively.

5. Retain as much of a word as possible on the first line; otherwise, retain at least two letters of a word on the first line.

6. Whenever possible, divide a word after its prefix or before its suffix: dis·or·gan·ize, set·tle·ment

   Preferred: dis·organize, settle·ment

7. Whenever possible, divide a compound word between the elements of the compound: busi·ness·woman, over·produc·tion

   Preferred: business·woman, over·production

8. Divide hyphenated words at the hyphen only: self-assured, sister-in-law

9. Divide words between double consonants when a suffix is added unless the root word itself ends in double letters, in which case division is made after the double letters: small·est, fill·ing, miss·ing, big·gest, con·trol·ling, mis·sion

10. Divide a word between two consecutive single-vowel syllables: con·tinu·ation, situ·ation

11. In general, retain an internal single-vowel with the first part of a word: sepa·rate, elimi·nate

    But, divide before a single-vowel if that syllable is part of the word ending forms of *able* or *ible, icle* or *ical, ity* or *ety:* pay·able, med·ical, abil·ity

    Also, divide before a single-vowel syllable if that syllable is part of a root word which contains a prefix: dis·agree, dis·avow

12. Retain the single vowel *i* with *za* in nouns ending in ization: or·gan·iza·tion, au·thor·iza·tion

    The reference source used for syllabication of words was *The American Heritage Dictionary of the English Language, New College Edition* (Houghton Mifflin Company, Boston).

A

a	.	academy	*acdre*
a.m.	*a*	ac·cel·era·tor	*lrar*
aban·doned	*abNn-*	ac·cept	*ac*
abey·ance	*abaN*	ac·cept·able	*acB*
abil·ities	*Bls*	ac·cep·tance	*acN*
abil·ity	*Bl*	ac·cepted	*ac-*
able	*B*	ac·cept·ing	*ac_*
ably	*Bl*	ac·cepts	*acs*
ab·nor·mal	*abnrl*	ac·cess	*vs*
aboard	*abrd*	ac·ces·so·ries	*vsres*
about	*ab*	ac·ci·dent	*vdN*
above	*abv*	ac·ci·den·tal	*vdNl*
abroad	*abrd*	ac·ci·dents	*vdNs*
ab·sence	*absN*	ac·com·mo·date	*akda*
ab·sences	*absNs*	ac·com·mo·dat·ing	*akda_*
ab·so·lute	*abslu*	ac·com·mo·da·tions	*akdjs*
ab·so·lutely	*abslul*	ac·com·pa·nied	*aco-*
ab·sorb	*absrb*	ac·com·pa·nies	*acos*
ab·stract	*absrc*	ac·com·pa·ni·ment	*acom*
abun·dant	*abNN*	ac·com·pa·nist	*acos*
aca·demic	*acdrc*	ac·com·pany	*aco*
		ac·com·pa·ny·ing	*aco_*
		ac·com·plish	*ak*

ac·com·plished	_ak-_	ac·cu·rate	_acrl_
ac·com·plish·ing	_ak_	ac·cu·rately	_acrll_
ac·com·plish·ment	_akm_	achieve	_aCv_
ac·com·plish·ments	_akms_	achieved	_aCv-_
ac·cord	_acrd_	achieve·ment	_aCvm_
ac·cord·ance	_acrdN_	achieve·ments	_aCvms_
ac·cord·ing	_acrd_	achiev·ing	_aCv_
ac·cord·ingly	_acrdl_	ac·knowl·edge	_acq_
ac·count	_ak_	ac·knowl·edged	_acq-_
ac·count·ant	_akN_	ac·knowl·edges	_acqs_
ac·count·ants	_akNs_	ac·knowl·edg·ing	_acq_
ac·count·ing	_ak_	ac·knowl·edg·ment	_acqm_
ac·counts	_aks_	ac·knowl·edg·ments	_acqms_
ac·credit	_acr_	ac·quaint	_aqN_
ac·credi·ta·tion	_acry_	ac·quain·tance	_aqNN_
ac·cred·ited	_acr-_	ac·quainted	_aqN-_
ac·cred·it·ing	_acr_	ac·quire	_aq_
ac·cred·its	_acrs_	ac·quired	_aq-_
ac·crued	_acru-_	ac·quir·ing	_aq-_
ac·cu·mu·late	_acla_	ac·qui·si·tion	_aqzl_
ac·cu·mu·lated	_acla-_	ac·qui·si·tions	_aqzls_
ac·cu·mu·la·tion	_acly_	acre	_acr_
ac·cu·racy	_acrse_	acre·age	_acry_

Word	Shorthand	Word	Shorthand
acres	*acrs*	ad·di·tional	*adyl*
across	*acrs*	ad·di·tion·ally	*adyll*
acrylic	*acrlc*	ad·di·tions	*adys*
act	*ac*	ad·dress	*adrs* (N. or V.) *Ars* (N.)
acted	*ac-*	ad·dressed	*adrs-*
act·ing	*ac*	ad·dresser	*adrsr*
ac·tion	*acy*	ad·dress·ers	*adrsrs*
ac·tions	*acys*	ad·dresses	*adrss* (N. or V.) *Arss* (N.)
ac·tive	*acv*	ad·dress·ing	*adrs*
ac·tively	*acvl*	adds	*As*
ac·tiv·ities	*acv ʿs*	ade·quate	*Aql*
ac·tiv·ity	*acv ʾ*	ade·quately	*Aqll*
acts	*acs*	ad·ja·cent	*aysN*
ac·tual	*acCul*	ad·joins	*ayyns*
ac·tu·ally	*acCull*	ad·just	*ayS*
ac·tu·arial	*acCurel*	ad·justed	*ayS-*
acute	*acu*	ad·juster	*aySr*
ad	*a*	ad·just·ers	*aySrs*
adapt·able	*adplB*	ad·just·ing	*ayS*
add	*a*	ad·just·ment	*aySm*
added	*a-*	ad·just·ments	*aySms*
add·ing	*a*	ad·min·is·ter	*Amsr*
ad·di·tion	*ady*	ad·min·is·tered	*Amsr-*

Word	Shorthand	Word	Shorthand
ad·min·is·ter·ing	*Amsr*	ad·vance·ment	*Avnm*
ad·min·is·trate	*Am*	ad·vances	*Avns*
ad·min·is·trates	*Ams*	ad·van·tage	*Avz*
ad·min·is·trat·ing	*Am*	ad·van·ta·geous	*Avzs*
ad·min·is·tra·tion	*Amy*	ad·van·tages	*Avzs*
ad·min·is·tra·tions	*Amys*	ad·verse	*Avrs*
ad·min·is·tra·tive	*Amv*	ad·versely	*Avrsl*
ad·min·is·tra·tor	*Amr*	ad·ver·tise	*Av*
ad·min·is·tra·tors	*Amrs*	ad·ver·tised	*Av-*
ad·mis·sion	*Ay*	ad·ver·tise·ment	*Avm*
ad·mis·sions	*Ays*	ad·ver·tise·ments	*Avms*
admit	*Al*	ad·ver·tiser	*Avr*
ad·mit·ted	*Al-*	ad·ver·tises	*Avs*
ado·les·cent	*Alsn*	ad·ver·tis·ing	*Av-*
ado·les·cents	*Alsns*	ad·vice	*Avs*
adopt	*adpl*	ad·vis·abil·ity	*Avzβ^l*
adopted	*adpl-*	ad·vis·able	*Avzβ*
adop·tion	*adpy*	ad·vise	*Avz*
ads	*As*	ad·vised	*Avz-*
adult	*adll*	ad·vises	*Avzs*
adults	*adlls*	ad·vis·ing	*Avz-*
ad·vance	*Avn*	ad·vi·sory	*Avzre*
ad·vanced	*Avn-*	aero·space	*arsps*

af·fairs	*afrs*	again	*ag*
af·fect	*afc*	against	*ag*
af·fected	*afc-*	age	*ay*
af·fect·ing	*afc_*	aged	*ay-*
af·fi·da·vit	*afdvt*	agen·cies	*ayNes*
af·fi·da·vits	*afdvts*	agency	*ayNe*
af·fili·ate	*aflä aflēt* v. N.	agenda	*ayNa*
af·fili·ated	*afla-*	agent	*ayN*
af·fili·ation	*afley*	agents	*ayNs*
af·fixed	*afx-*	ages	*ays*
af·ford	*afd*	ag·gre·gate	*agrgt agrga* adj. v.
af·forded	*afd-*	ago	*ag*
af·ford·ing	*afd_*	agree	*agre*
af·fords	*afds*	agree·able	*agreß*
afore·said	*afsd*	agreed	*agre-*
afraid	*afrd*	agree·ment	*agrem*
after	*af*	agree·ments	*agrems*
af·ter·math	*aft*	agrees	*agres*
af·ter·noon	*afnn*	ag·ri·cul·tural	*agrl*
af·ter·noons	*afnns*	ag·ri·cul·tur·ally	*agrll*
af·ter·thought	*aftt*	ag·ri·cul·ture	*agr*
af·ter·ward	*afw*	a·head	*ahd*
af·ter·wards	*afws*	aid	*ad*

aids	*ads*	al·lo·cated	*Aca-*
aim	*a*	al·lo·ca·tion	*Acy*
aimed	*a -*	al·lot·ment	*allm*
air	*ar*	al·lot·ted	*all-*
air·craft	*arcrft*	allow	*alo*
air·line	*arln*	al·low·able	*aloB*
air·lines	*arlns*	al·low·ance	*aloN*
air·port	*arpl*	al·low·ances	*aloNs*
air·ports	*arpls*	al·lowed	*alo-*
air·ways	*ar as*	al·low·ing	*alo*
alarm	*alr*	al·lows	*alos*
album	*Ab*	al·most	*A8*
al·bums	*Abs*	alone	*aln*
al·co·hol	*Achl*	along	*alg*
al·co·holic	*Achlc*	along·side	*algsd*
alert	*alrl*	al·pha·bet	*Afbl*
align·ment	*alnm*	al·ready	*Ar*
alive	*alv*	also	*Aso*
all	*A*	alter	*Alr*
al·le·vi·ate	*alva*	al·tera·tions	*Alrs*
alley	*Ae*	al·tered	*Alr-*
al·lied	*Ai-*	al·ter·nate	*Alrna Alrnl*
al·lo·cate	*Aca*	al·ter·na·tive	*Alrnv*

Word		Word	
al·ter·na·tives	*Alrnvs*	amounts	*a—ts*
al·though	*Alo*	ample	*a—pl*
alu·mi·num	*alm*	amus·ing	*a—z*
alumni	*almi*	an	*·*
al·ways	*a*	analy·ses	*anlsz*
am	*⌢*	analy·sis	*anlss*
ama·teur	*a—tr*	ana·lyze	*alz*
ama·teurs	*a—trs*	ana·lyzed	*alz-*
amaz·ing	*a—z*	ana·lyz·ing	*alz*
am·bas·sa·dor	*a—bsdr*	and	*+*
am·bi·tions	*a—bys*	angle	*agl*
am·bu·lance	*a—beN*	ani·mals	*a—ls*
amend	*am*	an·ni·ver·sary	*avrsre*
amended	*am-*	an·nounce	*anoN*
amend·ment	*amm*	an·nounced	*anoN-*
amend·ments	*amms*	an·nounce·ment	*anoNm*
America	*a*	an·nounce·ments	*anoNms*
American	*a*	an·nounc·ing	*anoN*
Americans	*ars*	an·noy·ance	*anyN*
among	*a—g*	an·nual	*aul*
amount	*a—t*	an·nu·ally	*aull*
amounted	*a—t-*	an·nu·ities	*anu⁶*
amount·ing	*a—t*	an·nu·ity	*anu¹*

annul	*anl*	apolo·gize	*aplyz*
an·other	*aol*	apology	*aplye*
an·swer	*asr*	ap·par·ent	*aprN*
an·swered	*asr-*	ap·par·ently	*aprNl*
an·swer·ing	*asr*	ap·peal	*apl*
an·swers	*asrs*	ap·peal·ing	*apl*
an·tici·pate	*alspa*	ap·peals	*apls*
an·tici·pated	*alspa-*	ap·pear	*apr*
an·tici·pa·tion	*alspy*	ap·pear·ance	*aprN*
an·tique	*alc*	ap·peared	*apr-*
anx·ious	*aqss*	ap·pear·ing	*apr*
any	*ne*	ap·pears	*aprs*
any·body	*nebde*	ap·pli·ance	*apliN*
any·how	*neho*	ap·pli·ances	*apliNs*
any·one	*ne1*	ap·pli·ca·ble	*aplcB*
any·thing	*ne*	ap·pli·cant	*aplcN*
any·time	*nel*	ap·pli·cants	*aplcNs*
any·way	*nea*	ap·pli·ca·tion	*aplcy*
any·where	*ner*	ap·pli·ca·tions	*aplcys*
apart	*apl*	ap·plied	*apli-*
apart·ment	*aplm*	ap·plies	*aplis*
apart·ments	*aplms*	apply	*apli*
apolo·gies	*aplyes*	ap·ply·ing	*apli*

Word	Shorthand	Word	Shorthand
ap·point	*apy*	ap·proved	*apv-*
ap·pointed	*apy-*	ap·proves	*apvs*
ap·point·ment	*apym*	ap·prov·ing	*apv_*
ap·point·ments	*apyms*	ap·proxi·mate	*apx*
ap·por·tion·ment	*aprym*	ap·proxi·mated	*apx-*
ap·praisal	*aprzl*	ap·proxi·mately	*apxl*
ap·praised	*aprz-*	ap·proxi·ma·tion	*apxy*
ap·pre·ci·ate	*ap*	ap·ti·tude	*aplld*
ap·pre·ci·ated	*ap-*	ar·bi·trary	*arblrre*
ap·pre·ci·ates	*aps*	ar·bi·tra·tion	*arblry*
ap·pre·cia·tion	*apy*	ar·chi·tect	*arclc*
ap·pre·cia·tive	*apv*	ar·chi·tects	*arclcs*
ap·proach	*aprC*	ar·chi·tec·tural	*arclcCrl*
ap·proaches	*aprCs*	are	*ɾ*
ap·proach·ing	*aprC_*	area	*ara*
ap·pro·pri·ate	*apo*	areas	*aras*
ap·pro·pri·ated	*apo-*	aren't	*ɾN*
ap·pro·pri·ately	*apol*	arena	*arna*
ap·pro·pri·at·ing	*apo_*	ar·gu·ment	*argum*
ap·pro·pria·tion	*apoy*	ar·gu·ments	*argums*
ap·pro·pria·tions	*apoys*	arise	*arz*
ap·proval	*apvl*	arises	*arzs*
ap·prove	*apv*	aris·ing	*arz_*

arm·chair	*arᴄr*	arts	*arts*
army	*arme*	as	*z*
around	*aroN*	as·cer·tain	*asrln*
ar·range	*ar*	ash	*aA*
ar·ranged	*ar-*	aside	*asd*
ar·range·ment	*arm*	ask	*asc*
ar·range·ments	*arms*	asked	*asc-*
ar·ranger	*arr*	ask·ing	*asc_*
ar·ranges	*ars*	as·pect	*aspc*
ar·rang·ing	*ar_*	as·pects	*aspcs*
ar·rears	*arrs*	as·phalt	*asfll*
ar·rest	*arS*	as·sem·bled	*as B-*
ar·ri·val	*arvl*	as·sem·blies	*as Bs*
ar·rive	*arv*	as·sem·bling	*as B_*
ar·rived	*arv-*	as·sem·bly	*as B*
ar·rives	*arvs*	as·sess	*ass*
ar·riv·ing	*arv_*	as·sessed	*ass-*
arrow	*aro*	as·sess·ment	*assm*
art	*arl*	as·sess·ments	*assms*
ar·ti·cle	*arlcl*	asset	*asl*
ar·ti·cles	*arlcls*	as·sets	*asls*
ar·ti·fi·cial	*arlfsl*	as·sign	*asn*
art·ists	*arlSs*	as·signed	*asn-*

Word	Shorthand	Word	Shorthand
as·sign·ing	*asn*	as·sured	*asr-*
as·sign·ment	*asnm*	as·sures	*asrs*
as·sign·ments	*asnms*	as·sur·ing	*asr*
as·sist	*ass*	asthma	*azɣa*
as·sis·tance	*assN*	asth·matic	*azɣc*
as·sis·tant	*assN*	at	*∕*
as·sis·tant·ship	*assN∕*	ath·letic	*allc*
as·sisted	*ass-*	atlas	*alls*
as·sist·ing	*ass*	at·mos·phere	*alɣsfr*
as·so·ci·ate	*aso*	atomic	*alc*
as·so·ci·ated	*aso-*	at·tach	*alC*
as·so·ci·ates	*asos*	at·tached	*alC-*
as·so·ci·at·ing	*aso*	at·taches	*alCs*
as·so·cia·tion	*asoɟ*	at·tach·ing	*alC*
as·so·cia·tions	*asoɟs*	at·tach·ment	*alCm*
as·sorted	*asrl-*	at·tack	*alc*
as·sume	*as*	at·tain·ing	*aln*
as·sumed	*as-*	at·tempt	*alɫ*
as·sumes	*ass*	at·tempted	*alɫ-*
as·sum·ing	*as*	at·tempt·ing	*alɫ*
as·sump·tion	*asɟ*	at·tempts	*alɫs*
as·sur·ance	*asrN*	at·tend	*alN*
as·sure	*asr*	at·ten·dance	*alNN*

at·tend·ed	_alM-_	au·thor·iza·tion	_alrzj_
at·tend·ing	_alM_	au·thor·ize	_alrz_
at·ten·tion	_all_	au·thor·ized	_alrz-_
at·ti·tude	_alld_	au·thor·iz·ing	_alrz_
at·ti·tudes	_allds_	au·thors	_alrs_
at·tor·ney	_alrne_	auto	_alo_
at·tor·neys	_alrnes_	au·to·mated	_alra-_
at·tract	_alrc_	au·to·matic	_alrlc_
at·tracted	_alrc-_	au·to·mat·ically	_alrlcl_
at·trac·tions	_alrcjs_	au·to·ma·tion	_alry_
at·trac·tive	_alrcv_	au·to·mo·bile	_aloB_
at·trib·ut·able	_alrbuB_	au·to·mo·biles	_aloBs_
au·di·ence	_adeM_	au·to·mo·tive	_alrv_
audit	_adl_	aux·il·iary	_agzlre_
au·dit·ing	_adl_	avail	_avl_
au·di·tor	_adlr_	avail·abil·ity	_avlB_
au·di·to·rium	_adlre_	avail·able	_avlB_
au·di·tors	_adlrs_	ave·nue	_ave_
au·dits	_adls_	ave·nues	_aves_
au·thor	_alr_	av·er·age	_avrj_
au·thori·ta·tive	_alrlv_	av·er·ages	_avrjs_
au·thor·ities	_alr ls_	av·er·ag·ing	_avrj-_
au·thor·ity	_alr l_	avia·tion	_avej_

avoid	*avyd*	badly	*bdl*
avoided	*avyd-*	bag	*bg*
await	*a a*	bag·gage	*bgj*
await·ing	*a a*	bags	*bgs*
award	*aw*	bake	*bc*
awarded	*aw-*	baked	*bc-*
awards	*aws*	bak·ery	*bcre*
aware	*a r*	bak·ing	*bc*
away	*a a*	bal·ance	*bln*
awe·some	*as*	bal·ances	*blns*
axle	*l*	bale	*bl*
		bales	*bls*
		ball	*bl*
B		balls	*bls*
		bank	*bg*
		bank·ers	*bgrs*
baby	*bbe*	bank·ing	*bg-*
back	*bc*	banks	*bgs*
backed	*bc-*	ban·ner	*bnr*
back·ground	*bcgron*	ban·quet	*bngl*
back·guard	*bcgrd*	bar	*br*
back·ing	*bc*	bar·ber	*brbr*
back·ward	*bcw*	bare	*br*
bad	*bd*		
badges	*bjs*		

bar·gain	*brgn*	bear	*br*
bar·gain·ing	*brgn_*	bear·ing	*br*
bark	*brc*	bear·ings	*br*
bar·rels	*brls*	bears	*brs*
bar·rier	*brer*	beat	*be*
bars	*brs*	beau·ti·ful	*blef*
base	*bo*	beau·ti·fully	*blefl*
based	*bo_*	beauty	*ble*
base·ment	*bsm*	bea·ver	*bvr*
bases	*bss* (N. or V.) *bsz* (N.)	be·came	*bk*
basic	*bsc*	be·cause	*bcz*
ba·si·cally	*bscl*	be·come	*bk*
basin	*bsn*	be·comes	*bks*
basis	*bss*	be·com·ing	*bk_*
batch	*bC*	bed	*bd*
bath	*bl*	bed·room	*bdr*
bat·ter·ies	*blres*	beds	*bds*
bat·tery	*blre*	beef	*bf*
bat·tle	*bll*	been	*b*
bay	*ba*	beer	*br*
be	*b*	beet	*be*
beach	*bC*	beets	*bes*
beans	*bns*	be·fore	*bf*

began	*bgn*	be·quests	*bqss*
begin	*bgn*	berths	*brts*
be·gin·ning	*bgn*	be·side	*bsd*
be·gins	*bgns*	best	*bs*
begun	*bgn*	bests	*bss*
be·half	*bhf*	bet·ter	*btr*
be·hind	*bhn*	be·tween	*btn*
being	*b*	bev·er·age	*bvrj*
be·lief	*blf*	bev·er·ages	*bvrjs*
be·lieve	*blv*	be·yond	*ben*
be·lieved	*blv-*	bib·li·og·ra·phy	*bblegrfe*
bell	*bl*	bid	*bd*
be·long·ing	*blg*	bid·der	*bdr*
below	*blo*	bid·ders	*bdrs*
belt	*blt*	bid·ding	*bd*
benches	*bncs*	bids	*bds*
bend	*bn*	big	*bg*
bene·fi·cial	*bnfsl*	big·ger	*bgr*
bene·fi·ci·ar·ies	*bnfseres*	big·gest	*bgs*
bene·fi·ci·ary	*bnfsere*	bill	*bl*
bene·fit	*bnfl*	billed	*bl-*
bene·fits	*bnfls*	bill·ing	*bl*
be·quest	*bqs*	bil·lion	*B*

bil·lion·aire	*Br*	blind	*blN*
bil·lions	*Bs*	block	*blc*
bil·lionth	*Bl*	blocks	*blcs*
bills	*bls*	blood	*bld*
bin	*bn*	blue	*blu*
binder	*bNr*	board	*brd*
bind·ing	*bN*	boards	*brds*
bio·graph·ical	*bigrfcl*	boat	*bo*
bi·og·ra·phy	*bigrfe*	boats	*bos*
bird	*brd*	bodily	*bdl*
birds	*brds*	body	*bde*
birth	*brl*	boil	*byl*
birth·day	*brld*	boiler	*bylr*
bit	*bl*	boil·ers	*bylrs*
bite	*br*	bolts	*blls*
bits	*bls*	bond	*bN*
black	*blc*	bond·ing	*bN*
blank	*blq*	bonds	*bNs*
blan·ket	*blql*	bone	*bn*
blan·kets	*blqls*	bonus	*bns*
blanks	*blqs*	book	*bc*
bless	*bls*	booked	*bc-*
blight	*bli*	book·ings	*bc=*

book·keep·ing	*bccp*	bowl	*bl*	
book·let	*bclt*	bowl·ing	*bl*	
book·lets	*bclls*	box	*bx*	
books	*bcs*	boxes	*bxs*	
boom	*b⌐*	boy	*by*	
booth	*bl*	boy·hood	*byh*	
booths	*bls*	boys	*bys*	
bor·der	*brdr*	branch	*brnc*	
bore	*br*	branches	*brncs*	
born	*brn*	brand	*brn*	
borne	*brn*	bread	*brd*	
bor·row	*bro*	break	*brc*	
bor·rowed	*bro-*	break·age	*brc*	
both	*bo*	break·down	*brcdon*	
bot·tle	*bll*	break·fast	*brcfs*	
bot·tles	*blls*	break·ing	*brc*	
bot·tom	*bl*	breaks	*brcs*	
bought	*bl*	breeder	*brdr*	
boule·vard	*blvd*	brew·ing	*bru*	
boule·vards	*blvds*	brick	*brc*	
bound	*boN*	bridge	*bry*	
bounda·ries	*boNres*	bridges	*brys*	
bow	*bo*	brief	*brf*	

briefly	*brfl*	budg·eted	*bjt-*
bright	*bri*	budg·ets	*bjts*
bring	*brg*	build	*bld*
bring·ing	*brg-*	build·ers	*bldrs*
brings	*brgs*	build·ing	*bld-*
broad	*brd*	build·ings	*bld=*
broad·cast	*brdc8*	built	*blt*
broader	*brdr*	bulbs	*blbs*
bro·chure	*brsr*	bulk	*blc*
bro·chures	*brsrs*	bul·le·tin	*blln*
bro·ken	*brcn*	bul·le·tins	*bllns*
bro·ker	*brcr*	bur·den	*brdn*
bro·kers	*brcrs*	bu·reau	*bro*
brother	*brlr*	bu·reaus	*bros*
broth·ers	*brlrs*	burned	*brn-*
brought	*brl*	burner	*brnr*
brown	*bron*	bus	*bs*
browse	*broz*	busi·ness	*bs*
brush	*brs*	busi·nesses	*bss*
bucket	*bcl*	busi·ness·like	*bslc*
buck·ets	*bcls*	busi·ness·man	*bs—m*
bud	*bd*	busi·ness·men	*bsm*
budget	*bjl*	busi·ness·woman	*bs—m*

busi·ness·women	*bs m*	cakes	*ccs*
busy	*bze*	cal·cu·late	*clcla*
but	*b*	cal·cu·lated	*clcla-*
but·ler	*bllr*	cal·cu·lat·ing	*clcla_*
but·ton	*bln*	cal·cu·la·tion	*clclj*
but·tons	*blns*	cal·cu·la·tor	*clclar*
buy	*b*	cal·en·dar	*clNr*
buyer	*br*	call	*cl*
buy·ers	*brs*	called	*cl-*
buy·ing	*b_*	call·ing	*cl_*
buys	*bs*	calls	*cls*
by	*b*	came	*k*
by·laws	*blas*	cam·era	*c ra*
by·pass	*bps*	camp	*c p*
		cam·paign	*c pn*

C

		camp·ing	*c p_*
		cam·pus	*c ps*
cabi·net	*cbnl*	can	*c*
cabi·nets	*cbnls*	can't	*cN*
cable	*cB*	Canadian	*cnden*
ca·ble·gram	*cBg*	canal	*cnl*
cafe·te·ria	*cflra*	can·cel	*csl*
cake	*cc*	can·celed	*csl-*

can·cel·ing	_csl_	cap·ture	_cpCr_
can·cel·la·tion	_csl̄_	car	_cr_
can·cel·la·tions	_csls_	car·bon	_crbn_
can·cer	_csr_	card	_crd_
can·did	_cdd_	card·board	_crdbrd_
can·di·date	_cdd̃l cdd̃a_	car·diac	_crdec_
can·di·dates	_cddls_	cards	_crds_
candy	_cde_	care	_cr_
cane	_cn_	ca·reer	_crr_
canned	_c-_	ca·reers	_crrs_
can·not	_cn_	care·ful	_crf_
cans	_cs_	care·fully	_crfl_
cap	_cp_	care·less·ness	_crls'_
ca·pa·bil·ities	_cpβls_	cargo	_crg_
ca·pa·bil·ity	_cpβl_	car·load	_crld_
ca·pa·ble	_cpβ_	car·pet	_crpt_
ca·pac·ity	_cps̸l_	car·pet·ing	_crpt̲_
capi·tal	_cpll_	car·port	_crpt_
capi·tol	_cpll_	car·ried	_cre-_
cap·tain	_cpln_	car·rier	_crer_
cap·tion	_cpʃ_	car·ri·ers	_crers_
cap·tioned	_cpʃ-_	car·ries	_cres_
cap·tions	_cpʃs_	carry	_cre_

car·ry·ing	*cre*	caused	*cz-*
cars	*crs*	causes	*czs*
car·ton	*crtn*	caus·ing	*cz-*
car·tons	*crtns*	ceil·ing	*slg*
car·toons	*crtns*	cele·bra·tion	*slbry*
case	*cs*	cell	*sl*
cases	*css*	Celsius	*slses*
cash	*cA*	ce·ment	*sm*
cashed	*cA-*	ceme·tery	*sdre*
cash·iers	*cArs*	cen·sus	*sNs*
cas·ing	*cs-*	cent	*¢*
cast	*cS*	cen·ter	*sNr*
casual	*czul*	cen·ters	*sNrs*
casu·alty	*czulle*	cen·tral	*sNrl*
cata·log	*cal*	cen·tral·ized	*sNrlz-*
cata·logs	*cals*	cen·trifu·gal	*sntrfgl*
catch	*cC*	cents	*¢*
cate·go·ries	*clgres*	cen·tury	*snCre*
cate·gory	*clgre*	cer·tain	*Stn*
cat·er·pil·lar	*clrplr*	cer·tainly	*Stnl*
cat·tle	*cll*	cer·tifi·cate	*Stfcl*
caught	*cl*	cer·tifi·cates	*Stfcls*
cause	*cz*	cer·ti·fi·ca·tion	*Stfy*

cer·ti·fied	*Slf-*	chapel	*Cpl*
cer·tify	*Slf*	chap·ter	*Cplr*
chain	*Cn*	chap·ters	*Cplrs*
chair	*Cr*	char·ac·ter	*crc*
chair·man	*Crm*	char·ac·ter·is·tic	*crc*
chair·men	*Crm*	char·ac·ter·is·ti·cally	*crcl*
chair·per·son	*CrPsn*	char·ac·ter·is·tics	*crcs*
chairs	*Crs*	char·ac·ter·iza·tion	*crczf*
chair·woman	*Cr m*	char·ac·ter·iza·tions	*crczfs*
chair·women	*Cr m*	char·ac·ter·ize	*crcz*
chal·lenge	*Clnj*	char·ac·ter·iz·ing	*crcz-*
chal·lenges	*Clnjs*	char·ac·ters	*crcs*
chal·leng·ing	*Clnj-*	charge	*G*
cham·ber	*Cbr*	charged	*G-*
cham·bers	*Cbrs*	charges	*Gs*
chance	*CN*	charg·ing	*G-*
chances	*CNs*	chari·ta·ble	*CrlB*
change	*Cnj*	chart	*Crl*
changed	*Cnj-*	char·ter	*Crlr*
changes	*Cnjs*	charts	*Crls*
chang·ing	*Cnj-*	chase	*Cs*
chan·nel	*Cnl*	cheaper	*Cpr*
chan·nels	*Cnls*	check	*Cc*

checked	_Cc -_	church	_CrC_
check·ing	_Cc_	churches	_CrCs_
checks	_Ccs_	ciga·rette	_sgrt_
chem·ical	_c rcl_	cir·cle	_Scl_
chem·icals	_c rcls_	cir·cuit	_Scl_
chem·is·try	_c Sre_	cir·cuits	_Scls_
cherry	_Cre_	cir·cu·lar	_Sclr_
chest	_CS_	cir·cu·lat·ing	_Scla_
chief	_Cf_	cir·cu·la·tion	_Sclj_
child	_Cld_	cir·cum·stance	_Sk_
child·hood	_Cldh_	cir·cum·stances	_Sks_
chil·dren	_Cldrn_	cir·cum·stan·tial	_Sksl_
chilled	_Cl -_	cite	_st_
chips	_Cps_	cit·ies	_stes_
choco·late	_Ccll_	citi·zen	_stzn_
choice	_Cys_	citi·zens	_stzns_
choices	_Cyss_	cit·rus	_strs_
choose	_Cz_	city	_ste_
choos·ing	_Cz-_	civic	_svc_
chose	_Cz_	civil	_svl_
cho·sen	_Czn_	ci·vil·ian	_svlyn_
Christmas	_Xns_	ci·vil·ians	_svlyns_
Christmases	_Xnss_	civi·li·za·tion	_svlzj_

claim	*cl*	clear	*clr*
claim·ant	*clm*	clear·ance	*clrn*
claimed	*cl-*	cleared	*clr-*
claim·ing	*cl*	clear·ing	*clr*
claims	*cls*	clearly	*clrl*
clari·fi·ca·tion	*clrf*	cler·ical	*clrcl*
clari·fied	*clrf-*	clerk	*clrc*
clarify	*clrf*	clerks	*clrcs*
clari·fy·ing	*clrf*	clever	*clvr*
class	*cls*	cli·ent	*cln*
classes	*clss*	cli·ents	*clns*
clas·si·fi·ca·tion	*clsf*	cli·mate	*cld*
clas·si·fi·ca·tions	*clsfs*	clinic	*clnc*
clas·si·fied	*clsf-*	clin·ical	*clncl*
class·room	*clsr*	clock	*clc*
class·rooms	*clsrs*	close	*cls* adj. *clz* v.
clause	*clz*	closed	*clz-*
clay	*cla*	closely	*clsl*
clean	*cln*	closer	*clsr*
cleaned	*cln-*	closes	*clzs*
cleaner	*clnr*	closet	*clzt*
clean·ers	*clnrs*	clos·ing	*clz*
clean·ing	*cln*	cloth	*clt*

cloth·ing	*cll*	col·lect	*clc*
club	*clb*	col·lected	*clc-*
clubs	*clbs*	col·lect·ing	*clc*
clus·ter	*clsr*	col·lec·tion	*clcy*
coach	*cc*	col·lec·tions	*clcys*
coal	*cl*	col·lec·tively	*clcvl*
coast	*cs*	col·lege	*cly*
coat	*co*	col·leges	*clys*
coated	*co-*	col·li·sion	*cly*
coat·ing	*co*	color	*clr*
coat·ings	*co*	col·or·ful	*clrf*
coats	*cos*	col·ors	*clrs*
coat·tail	*coll*	col·umn	*cl*
code	*cd*	col·umns	*cls*
coded	*cd-*	com·bi·na·tion	*kbny*
codes	*cds*	com·bi·na·tions	*kbnys*
cod·ing	*cd*	com·bine	*kbn*
cof·fee	*cfe*	com·bined	*kbn-*
coil	*cyl*	come	*k*
cold	*cld*	comes	*ks*
col·lat·eral	*cllrl*	com·fort	*kfl*
col·league	*clg*	com·fort·able	*kflB*
col·leagues	*clgs*	com·ing	*k*

Word	Outline	Word	Outline
com·mand	*kM*	com·mod·ity	*kd^l*
com·mence	*kM*	com·mon	*kn*
com·mence·ment	*kMm*	com·mon·wealth	*kn ll*
com·menc·ing	*kM*	com·mu·ni·cate	*knca*
com·mend	*kM*	com·mu·ni·ca·tion	*kncy*
com·men·su·rate	*kMrl*	com·mu·ni·ca·tions	*kncys*
com·ment	*kM*	com·mu·ni·ties	*kn^ls*
com·mented	*kM-*	com·mu·ni·ty	*kn^l*
com·ment·ing	*kM*	com·pact	*kpc*
com·ments	*kMs*	com·pa·nies	*cos*
com·merce	*krs*	com·pan·ion	*kpnyn*
com·mer·cial	*krsl*	com·pan·ion·ship	*kpnyns*
com·mer·cials	*krsls*	com·pany	*co*
com·mis·sion	*kj*	com·pa·ra·ble	*kprB*
com·mis·sioner	*kjr*	com·para·tive	*kprv*
com·mis·sion·ers	*kjrs*	com·pare	*kpr*
com·mis·sions	*kjs*	com·pared	*kpr-*
com·mit·ment	*klm*	com·pari·son	*kprsn*
com·mit·ments	*klms*	com·part·ment	*kplm*
com·mit·ted	*kl-*	com·part·ments	*kplms*
com·mit·tee	*k*	com·pat·ible	*kplB*
com·mit·tees	*ks*	com·pen·sate	*kpNa*
com·mod·ities	*kd^ls*	com·pen·sa·tion	*kpN*

Word	Outline	Word	Outline
com·pete	kpe	com·pli·men·tary	kplmre
com·pe·tent	kplN	com·pli·ments	kplms
com·pe·ti·tion	kply	com·ply	kpli
com·peti·tive	kplv	com·ply·ing	kpli
com·pile	kpl	com·po·nents	kpnNs
com·piled	kpl-	com·posed	kpz-
com·pil·ing	kpl	com·pounded	kpoN-
com·plain	kpln	com·pre·hen·sive	kprhNv
com·plaint	kplN	com·pres·sor	kprsr
com·plaints	kplNs	com·pres·sors	kprsrs
com·ple·ment	kplm	com·pro·mise	kprz
com·plete	kp	comp·trol·ler	klr
com·pleted	kp-	com·pu·ta·tion	kply
com·pletely	kpl	com·pu·ta·tions	kplys
com·plete·ness	kp'	com·pute	kpu
com·pletes	kps	com·puted	kpu-
com·plet·ing	kp	com·puter	kpur
com·ple·tion	kpy	com·put·ers	kpurs
com·plex	kplx	com·put·ing	kpu
com·pli·ance	kplN	con·ceal	ksl
com·pli·cated	kplca-	con·cealed	ksl-
com·plied	kpli-	con·ceiv·able	ksvb
com·pli·ment	kplm	con·cen·trated	ksNra-

con·cept	*kspt*	con·duct	*kdc*
con·cepts	*kspts*	con·ducted	*kdc-*
con·cern	*ksrn*	con·duct·ing	*kdc̲*
con·cerned	*ksrn-*	con·duc·tor	*kdcr*
con·cern·ing	*ksrn̲*	con·fer·ence	*kfrN*
con·cerns	*ksrns*	con·fer·ences	*kfrNs*
con·certed	*ksrt-*	con·ferred	*kfr-*
con·ces·sion	*ksj*	con·fi·dence	*kfdN*
con·ces·sions	*ksjs*	con·fi·dent	*kfdN*
con·clude	*kcld*	con·fi·den·tial	*kfdnsl*
con·cluded	*kcld-*	con·fi·dently	*kfdNl*
con·clu·sion	*kclj*	con·fined	*kfn-*
con·clu·sions	*kcljs*	con·fine·ment	*kfnm*
con·crete	*kcre*	con·firm	*kfr*
con·cur	*kcr*	con·fir·ma·tion	*kfrj*
con·cur·rence	*kcrN*	con·firmed	*kfr-*
con·cur·ring	*kcr̲*	con·firm·ing	*kfr̲*
con·densed	*kd̄N-*	con·firms	*kfrs*
con·denser	*kd̄Nr*	con·flict	*kflc*
con·di·tion	*kdj*	con·flicts	*kflcs*
con·di·tional	*kdjl*	con·form	*kf*
con·di·tion·ing	*kdj̲*	con·formed	*kf-*
con·di·tions	*kdjs*	con·form·ing	*kf̲*

con·forms	*kfns*	con·ser·va·tive	*ksrvv*
con·fuse	*kfz*	con·sider	*ks*
con·fused	*kfz-*	con·sid·er·able	*ksℓ*
con·fus·ing	*kfz-*	con·sid·er·ably	*ksℓ*
con·fu·sion	*kfj*	con·sid·er·ate	*ksℓ*
con·ges·tion	*kjsq*	con·sid·era·tion	*ksq*
con·gratu·late	*kq*	con·sid·era·tions	*ksqs*
con·gratu·la·tions	*kgjs*	con·sid·ered	*ks-*
con·gress	*kgrs*	con·sid·er·ing	*ks*
con·gres·sional	*kgryl*	con·sid·ers	*kss*
con·gress·man	*kgrs m*	con·signee	*ksne*
con·gress·wom·an	*kgrs m*	con·sist	*ksℓ*
con·junc·tion	*kjqy*	con·sisted	*ksℓ-*
con·nect	*kc*	con·sis·tent	*ksℓn*
con·nected	*kc-*	con·sis·tently	*ksℓnℓ*
con·nec·tion	*kcy*	con·sist·ing	*ksℓ*
con·nec·tions	*kcys*	con·sists	*ksℓs*
con·scious·ness	*kss'*	con·soli·dated	*ksℓda-*
con·sen·sus	*ksns*	con·stant	*ksn*
con·sent	*ksn*	con·stantly	*ksnℓ*
con·se·quence	*ksqn*	con·stitu·ent	*ksCun*
con·se·quently	*ksqnℓ*	con·sti·tute	*ksℓu*
con·ser·va·tion	*ksrvq*	con·sti·tutes	*ksℓus*

Word	Shorthand	Word	Shorthand
con·sti·tu·tion	*kSly*	con·tainer	*klnr*
con·sti·tu·tional	*kSlyl*	con·tain·ers	*klnrs*
con·struct	*kSrc*	con·tain·ing	*kln*
con·structed	*kSrc-*	con·tains	*klns*
con·struct·ing	*kSrc*	con·tami·na·tion	*klmy*
con·struc·tion	*kSrcy*	con·tem·plate	*kt͞pla*
con·struc·tive	*kSrcv*	con·tem·plated	*kt͞pla-*
con·sult	*ksll*	con·tem·plat·ing	*kt͞pla*
con·sult·ant	*ksllN*	con·tem·po·rary	*kt͞prre*
con·sult·ants	*ksllNs*	con·tent	*klN*
con·sul·ta·tion	*kslly*	con·tents	*klNs*
con·sulted	*ksll-*	con·test	*klS*
con·sult·ing	*ksll*	con·tests	*klSs*
con·sumer	*ks͞r*	con·ti·nen·tal	*klnNl*
con·sum·ers	*ks͞rs*	con·tin·gent	*klnyN*
con·sum·mate	*ks͞a* (v.) *ks͞l* (adj.)	con·tinual	*kul*
con·sump·tion	*ks͞y*	con·tinu·ally	*kull*
con·tact	*klc*	con·tinu·ation	*kuy*
con·tacted	*klc-*	con·tinue	*ku*
con·tact·ing	*klc*	con·tin·ued	*ku-*
con·tacts	*klcs*	con·tin·ues	*kus*
con·tain	*kln*	con·tinu·ing	*ku*
con·tained	*kln-*	con·ti·nu·ity	*ku^l*

con·tinu·ous	*kus*	con·trol·lers	*klrs*
con·tinu·ously	*kusl*	con·trol·ling	*kl*
con·tinuum	*ku*	con·trols	*kls*
con·tract	*kc*	con·tro·ver·sial	*klrvrsl*
con·tracted	*kc-*	con·ven·ience	*kv*
con·tract·ing	*kc*	con·ven·iences	*kvs*
con·trac·tor	*kcr*	con·ven·ient	*kv*
con·trac·tors	*kcrs*	con·ven·iently	*kvl*
con·tracts	*kcs*	con·ven·tion	*kvny*
con·trac·tual	*kcul*	con·ven·tional	*kvnyl*
con·trary	*klrre*	con·ven·tions	*kvnys*
con·trib·ute	*kb*	con·ver·sa·tion	*kvrsy*
con·trib·uted	*kb-*	con·ver·sa·tions	*kvrsys*
con·trib·utes	*kbs*	con·ver·sion	*kvry*
con·trib·ut·ing	*kb*	con·vert	*kvrl*
con·tri·bu·tion	*kby*	con·verted	*kvrl-*
con·tri·bu·tions	*kbys*	con·vert·ible	*kvrlB*
con·tribu·tor	*kbr*	con·vert·ing	*kvrl*
con·tribu·tors	*kbrs*	con·vey	*kva*
con·tribu·tory	*kbre*	con·vey·ance	*kvaN*
con·trol	*kl*	con·veyor	*kvar*
con·trolled	*kl-*	con·vic·tion	*kvcy*
con·trol·ler	*klr*	con·vince	*kvN*

Word	Outline	Word	Outline
con·vinced	kvN-	cor·dially	cryll
cook	cc	core	cr
cook·ing	cc	corn	crn
cool·ers	clrs	cor·ner	crnr
cool·ing	cl	cor·ners	crnrs
co·op·er·ate	cop	cor·po·rate	crprl
co·op·er·ated	cop-	cor·po·ra·tion	corp
co·op·er·ates	cops	cor·po·ra·tions	corps
co·op·er·at·ing	cop_	corps	cr
co·op·era·tion	copy	cor·rect	crc
co·op·era·tive	copv	cor·rected	crc-
co·op·era·tively	copvl	cor·rec·tion	crcy
co·op·era·tives	copvs	cor·rec·tional	crcyl
co·or·di·nate	cordna (v.) cordnl (adj. or N.)	cor·rec·tions	crcys
co·or·di·nated	cordna-	cor·rec·tive	crcv
co·or·di·na·tion	cordny	cor·rectly	crcl
co·or·di·na·tor	cordnar	cor·re·spond	cor
copier	cper	cor·re·sponded	cor-
cop·ies	cpes	cor·re·spon·dence	cor
cop·per	cpr	cor·re·spon·dent	corN
copy	cpe	cor·re·spon·dents	corNs
copy·ing	cpe_	cor·re·spond·ing	cor_
cor·dial	cryl	cor·re·sponds	cors

cor·ro·sion	_cry_	cou·ple	_cpl_
cost	_cS_	cou·ples	_cpls_
cost·ing	_cS_	cou·pon	_cpn_
costly	_cSl_	cou·pons	_cpns_
costs	_cSs_	course	_crs_
cot·ton	_cln_	courses	_crss_
could	_cd_	court	_crl_
couldn't	_cdN_	cour·te·sies	_crlses_
coun·cil	_ksl_	cour·tesy	_crlse_
coun·sel	_ksl_	courts	_crls_
coun·sel·ing	_ksl_	cover	_cvr_
coun·selor	_kslr_	cov·er·age	_cvry_
coun·sel·ors	_kslrs_	cov·er·ages	_cvrys_
count	_k_	cov·ered	_cvr -_
counter	_kr_	cov·er·ing	_cvr_
coun·ter·part	_krpl_	cov·ers	_cvrs_
count·ers	_krs_	cracked	_crc -_
coun·ties	_kes_	crafts	_crfls_
count·ing	_k_	cre·ate	_cra_
count·less	_kls_	cre·ated	_cra -_
coun·tries	_cNres_	cre·ates	_cras_
coun·try	_cNre_	cre·at·ing	_cra_
county	_ke_	crea·tive	_crav_

Word	Shorthand	Word	Shorthand
cre·den·tials	*crdnsls*	crys·tal	*crSl*
credit	*cr*	cubic	*cbc*
cred·it·able	*crB*	cues	*cus*
cred·ited	*cr-*	cuffs	*cfs*
cred·it·ing	*cr_*	cul·tural	*clCrl*
credi·tor	*crs*	cul·ture	*clCr*
credi·tors	*crrs*	curb	*crb*
cred·its	*crs*	cure	*cr*
creek	*crc*	cured	*cr-*
crew	*cru*	cur·ing	*cr_*
crews	*crus*	cu·ri·ous	*cres*
crip·pled	*crpl-*	cur·ren·cies	*crMes*
cri·sis	*crss*	cur·rency	*crMe*
cri·te·ria	*crlra*	cur·rent	*crM*
crit·ical	*crlcl*	cur·rently	*crMl*
crit·ics	*crlcs*	cur·ricu·lum	*crcl*
crop	*crp*	cus·tom	*cS*
crops	*crps*	cus·tom·arily	*cSrl*
cross	*crs*	cus·tomer	*K*
crossed	*crs-*	cus·tom·ers	*Ks*
cross·ing	*crs_*	cus·toms	*cSs*
crude	*crd*	cut	*cl*
cru·sade	*crsd*	cute	*cu*

cut·ting	_cl_	dates	_das_
cycle	_scl_	daugh·ter	_dlr_
cy·cles	_scls_	daugh·ters	_dlrs_
cyl·in·der	_slNr_	day	_d_
cyl·in·ders	_slNrs_	day·break	_dbrc_
		day·dream	_ddr_
		day·light	_dli_
D		days	_ds_
		day·time	_dl_
dai·lies	_dls_	dead	_dd_
daily	_dl_	dead·line	_ddln_
dairy	_dre_	deaf	_df_
dam·age	_dy_	deal	_dl_
dam·aged	_dy-_	dealer	_dlr_
dam·ages	_dys_	deal·ers	_dlrs_
dance	_dN_	deal·ing	_dl_
dan·ger	_dnjr_	deal·ings	_dl_
dan·ger·ous	_dnjrs_	deals	_dls_
dan·gers	_dnjrs_	dealt	_dll_
dark	_drc_	dean	_dn_
dar·ling	_drlg_	death	_dl_
data	_dla_	de·bate	_dba_
date	_da_	de·ben·tures	_dbnCrs_
dated	_da-_		

Word	Outline	Word	Outline
debts	*dls*	de·duct·ing	*ddc*
dec·ade	*dcd*	de·duc·tion	*ddcy*
de·ceased	*dss-*	de·duc·tions	*ddcys*
de·cide	*dsd*	deed	*dd*
de·cided	*dsd-*	deemed	*d~-*
de·ci·sion	*dsy*	deep	*dp*
de·ci·sions	*dsys*	deep·est	*dpß*
de·ci·sive	*dssv*	deeply	*dpl*
deck	*dc*	de·fect	*dfc*
decks	*dcs*	de·fec·tive	*dfcv*
dec·la·ra·tion	*dclr*	de·fects	*dfcs*
dec·la·ra·tions	*dclrs*	de·fen·dant	*dfNN*
de·clared	*dclr-*	de·fen·dants	*dfNNs*
de·cline	*dcln*	de·fense	*dfN*
de·clined	*dcln-*	defer	*dfr*
deco·rat·ing	*dcra*	de·fer·ment	*dfrm*
de·crease	*dcrs*	de·ferred	*dfr-*
de·creased	*dcrs-*	defi·cit	*dfsl*
dedi·cated	*ddca-*	de·fine	*dfn*
dedi·ca·tion	*ddcy*	de·fined	*dfn-*
de·duct	*ddc*	defi·nite	*dfnl*
de·ducted	*ddc-*	defi·nitely	*dfnll*
de·duct·ible	*ddcß*	defi·ni·tion	*dfny*

Word	Shorthand	Word	Shorthand
de·gree	*dgre*	de·luxe	*dlx*
delay	*dla*	de·mand	*dm*
de·layed	*dla-*	de·mand·ing	*dm_*
de·lays	*dlas*	de·mands	*dms*
dele·gate	*dlğa dlğl*	dem·on·strate	*dmSra*
dele·gated	*dlga-*	dem·on·strated	*dmSra-*
dele·gates	*dlğas dlğls*	dem·on·strates	*dmSras*
de·lete	*dle*	dem·on·stra·tion	*dmSry*
de·leted	*dle-*	dem·on·stra·tions	*dmSrys*
de·le·tion	*dly*	de·nial	*dnil*
de·light	*dli*	de·nied	*dni-*
de·lighted	*dli-*	den·sity	*dNL*
de·light·ful	*dlif*	den·tal	*dNl*
de·lin·quency	*dlqNe*	deny	*dni*
de·lin·quent	*dlqN*	de·part	*dpl*
de·liver	*dl*	de·part·ment	*dpl*
de·liv·er·ance	*dlN*	de·part·men·tal	*dpll*
de·liv·ered	*dl-*	de·part·men·tal·iza·tion	*dpllzy*
de·liv·er·ies	*dles*	de·part·men·tal·ize	*dpllz*
de·liv·er·ing	*dl_*	de·part·men·tal·izes	*dpllzs*
de·liv·ers	*dls*	de·part·ments	*dpls*
de·liv·ery	*dle*	de·parts	*dpls*
delta	*dlla*	de·par·ture	*dplr*

de·pend	*dpN*	deputy	*dple*
de·pend·able	*dpNB*	de·rided	*drd-*
de·pend·ent	*dpNN*	de·rived	*drv-*
de·pend·ents	*dpNNs*	de·scribe	*dS*
de·pend·ing	*dpN*	de·scribed	*dS-*
de·pends	*dpNs*	de·scribes	*dSs*
de·pleted	*dple-*	de·scrib·ing	*dS*
de·port	*dpl*	de·scrip·tion	*dSy*
de·por·ta·tion	*dply*	de·scrip·tions	*dSys*
de·por·ta·tions	*dplys*	de·scrip·tive	*dSv*
de·ported	*dpl-*	de·serve	*dzrv*
de·port·ing	*dpl*	de·serves	*dzrvs*
de·port·ment	*dplm*	de·serv·ing	*dzrv*
de·ports	*dpls*	de·sign	*dzn*
de·posit	*dpzl*	des·ig·nate	*dz̆gna dz̆g̈nl*
de·pos·ited	*dpzl-*	des·ig·nated	*dzgna-*
depo·si·tion	*dpzy*	des·ig·nat·ing	*dzgna*
de·pos·its	*dpzls*	des·ig·na·tion	*dzgny*
depot	*dpo*	de·signed	*dzn-*
de·pre·cia·tion	*dprsey*	de·signs	*dzns*
de·pres·sion	*dpry*	de·sir·able	*dzrB*
dep·ri·va·tion	*dprvy*	de·sire	*dzr*
depth	*dpl*	de·sired	*dzr-*

de·sires	dzrs	de·vel·op·ers	dvrs
de·sir·ous	dzrs	de·vel·op·ing	dv_
desk	dsc	de·vel·op·ment	dvm
desks	dscs	de·vel·op·mental	dvml
de·spite	dspi	de·vel·op·ment·ally	dvmll
des·ti·na·tion	dSny	de·vel·op·ments	dvms
de·stroy	dSry	de·vel·ops	dvs
de·stroyed	dSry-	de·vice	dvs
de·tail	dll	de·vices	dvss
de·tailed	dll-	de·vise	dvz
de·tails	dlls	de·vises	dvzs
de·tect	dlc	de·vote	dvo
de·tec·tion	dlcy	de·voted	dvo-
de·ter·gent	dlrgn	dia·be·tes	dibls
de·te·rio·ra·tion	dlrery	di·ag·no·sis	dignss
de·ter·mi·na·tion	dly	dia·gram	dig
de·ter·mine	dl	dial	dil
de·ter·mined	dl-	di·ame·ter	di—lr
de·ter·mines	dls	dia·mond	dmd
de·ter·min·ing	dl_	dic·tat·ing	dcla
de·velop	dv	dic·ta·tion	dcly
de·vel·oped	dv-	dic·tion·ary	dcyre
de·vel·oper	dvr	did	dd

didn't	*ddN*	di·rec·tion	*dry*
die	*di*	di·rec·tions	*drys*
died	*di-*	di·rec·tive	*drv*
dies	*dis*	di·rec·tives	*drvs*
die·sel	*dsl*	di·rectly	*drl*
diet	*dil*	di·rec·tor	*drr*
dif·fer·ence	*dfrN*	di·rec·to·ries	*drres*
dif·fer·ences	*dfrNs*	di·rec·tors	*drrs*
dif·fer·ent	*dfrN*	di·rec·tory	*drre*
dif·fi·cult	*dfc*	dis·abil·ity	*DBl*
dif·fi·cul·ties	*dfces*	dis·abled	*DB-*
dif·fi·culty	*dfce*	dis·ad·van·tage	*Davy*
di·gest	*dyS*	dis·ap·pear	*Dapr*
dili·gent	*dlyN*	dis·ap·pear·ance	*DaprN*
dili·gently	*dlyNl*	dis·ap·point	*Dapy*
di·men·sions	*dmys*	dis·ap·pointed	*Dapy-*
din·ing	*dn*	dis·ap·point·ment	*Dapym*
din·ner	*dnr*	dis·ap·proval	*Dapvl*
di·ploma	*dpl a*	dis·ap·prove	*Dapv*
di·plo·mas	*dpl as*	dis·ap·proved	*Dapv-*
di·rect	*dr*	dis·ap·proves	*Dapvs*
di·rected	*dr-*	dis·ap·prov·ing	*Dapv*
di·rect·ing	*dr*	dis·as·ter	*dzSr*

disc	*Dc*	dis·eases	*dzzs*
dis·charge	*Dcy*	dis·may	*Dra*
dis·charged	*Dcy-*	dis·or·gan·iza·tion	*Dogj*
dis·charg·ing	*Dcy_*	dis·or·gan·ize	*Doq*
dis·close	*Dclz*	dis·or·gan·ized	*Doq-*
dis·closes	*Dclzs*	dis·patcher	*Dpcr*
dis·clo·sure	*Dclzr*	dis·play	*Dpla*
dis·com·fort	*Dkfl*	dis·played	*Dpla-*
dis·con·tinue	*Dku*	dis·play·ing	*Dpla_*
dis·con·tin·ued	*Dku-*	dis·plays	*Dplas*
dis·con·tinu·ing	*Dku_*	dis·please	*Dp*
dis·count	*Dk*	dis·pleased	*Dp-*
dis·counts	*Dks*	dis·pleases	*Dps*
dis·cover	*Dcvr*	dis·posal	*Dpzl*
dis·cov·ered	*Dcvr-*	dis·pose	*Dpz*
dis·cre·tion	*Dcry*	dis·posed	*Dpz-*
dis·cuss	*Dcs*	dis·pos·ing	*Dpz_*
dis·cussed	*Dcs-*	dis·po·si·tion	*Dpzj*
dis·cusses	*Dcss*	dis·prove	*Dpv*
dis·cuss·ing	*Dcs_*	dis·proved	*Dpv-*
dis·cus·sion	*Dcy*	dis·proves	*Dpvs*
dis·cus·sions	*Dcjs*	dis·pute	*Dpu*
dis·ease	*dzz*	dis·re·gard	*Dre*

Word	Shorthand	Word	Shorthand
dis·sat·is·fac·tion	*Dsaty*	di·ver·si·fi·ca·tion	*dvrsff*
dis·tance	*DIN*	di·vided	*dvd-*
dis·tinct	*Dlq*	divi·dend	*dvdN*
dis·tinc·tive	*Dlqv*	divi·dends	*dvdNs*
dis·tin·guish	*Dlq s*	di·vides	*dvds*
dis·tin·guished	*Dlq s-*	di·vid·ing	*dvd_*
dis·trib·ute	*D*	di·vi·sion	*dvy*
dis·trib·uted	*D-*	di·vi·sions	*dvys*
dis·trib·utes	*Ds*	do	*du*
dis·trib·ut·ing	*D_*	dock	*dc*
dis·tri·bu·tion	*Dy*	docket	*dcl*
dis·tri·bu·tions	*Dys*	doc·tor	*dr*
dis·tribu·tive	*Dv*	doc·toral	*drl*
dis·tribu·tor	*Dr*	doc·tor·ate	*drl*
dis·tribu·tors	*Drs*	doc·tored	*dr-*
dis·tribu·tor·ship	*Drs*	doc·tor·ing	*dr_*
dis·trict	*Dlrc*	doc·tors	*drs*
dis·tricts	*Dlrcs*	docu·ment	*dcm*
dis·turb	*Dlrb*	docu·ments	*dcms*
dis·turbed	*Dlrb-*	does	*dz*
ditch	*dC*	doesn't	*dzN*
ditches	*dCs*	dog	*dq*
ditto	*dlo*	doing	*du_*

dol·lar	*$*	drain	*drn*
dol·lars	*$*	drain·age	*drny*
do·mes·tic	*d sc*	drama	*dr a*
don't	*dN*	dra·matic	*dr sc*
do·nated	*dna-*	draw	*dra*
do·na·tion	*dny*	draw·ing	*dra*
done	*dn*	draw·ings	*dra*
donor	*dnr*	drawn	*drn*
door	*dr*	dress	*drs*
doors	*drs*	dress·ing	*drs*
dose	*ds*	drill	*drl*
dou·ble	*dB*	drilled	*drl-*
dou·bled	*dB-*	drill·ing	*drl*
doubt	*dol*	drills	*drls*
doubted	*dol-*	drinks	*drqs*
doubt·ful	*dolf*	drive	*drv*
down	*don*	driven	*drvn*
down·hill	*donhl*	driver	*drvr*
down·town	*donton*	driv·ers	*drvrs*
down·ward	*donw*	driv·ing	*drv*
dozen	*dzn*	drop	*drp*
draft	*drfl*	dropped	*drp-*
drafts	*drfls*	drop·ping	*drp*

Word	Outline	Word	Outline		Outline
drops	*drps*			**E**	
drug	*drg*				
drums	*drᵤs*	each	*ec*		
dry	*dru*	eager	*egr*		
dual	*dul*	ear	*er*		
ducts	*dcs*	ear·lier	*erlr*		
due	*du*	ear·li·est	*erlS*		
dues	*dus*	early	*erl*		
duly	*dul*	earn	*ern*		
dump	*d⌐p*	earned	*ern-*		
dun	*dn*	ear·nestly	*ernSl*		
du·pli·cate	*dplct* ᵃᵈʲ· *dplca* ᵛ·	earn·ing	*ern_*		
du·pli·cated	*dplca-*	earn·ings	*ern=*		
du·pli·cat·ing	*dplca_*	earth	*erl*		
du·pli·ca·tion	*dplcj*	ease	*ez*		
du·pli·ca·tors	*dplcars*	ease·ment	*ezm*		
du·ra·ble	*drß*	easier	*ezer*		
du·ra·tion	*dry*	easily	*ezl*		
dur·ing	*du_*	east	*E*		
du·ties	*dtes*	east·erly	*Erl*		
duty	*dte*	east·ern	*Ern*		
dwell·ing	*dl_*	east·ward	*Ew*		
dy·namic	*dn⌐c*	easy	*eze*		

eat	*el*	ef·fec·tive	*efcv*
eco·nomic	*eco*	ef·fec·tively	*efcvl*
eco·nom·ical	*ecol*	ef·fec·tive·ness	*efcv'*
eco·nom·ically	*ecoll*	ef·fects	*efcs*
eco·nom·ics	*ecos*	ef·fi·ciency	*efsNe*
econo·mies	*ecos*	ef·fi·cient	*efsN*
econo·mist	*ecos*	ef·fi·ciently	*efsNl*
econo·mists	*ecoSs*	ef·fort	*efl*
economy	*eco*	ef·forts	*efls*
edit	*edl*	egg	*eq*
ed·ited	*edl-*	eggs	*egs*
edi·tion	*edy*	ei·ther	*elr*
edi·tions	*edys*	elder	*eldr*
edi·tor	*edlr*	elect	*elc*
edi·to·rial	*edlrel*	elected	*elc-*
edi·tors	*edlrs*	elec·tion	*elcy*
edu·cate	*eyca*	elec·tric	*elc*
edu·ca·tion	*eycy*	elec·tri·cal	*elcl*
edu·ca·tional	*eycyl*	elec·tri·cian	*ely*
edu·ca·tor	*eycar*	elec·tric·ity	*els'*
edu·ca·tors	*eycars*	elec·tron	*eln*
ef·fect	*efc*	elec·tronic	*elnc*
ef·fected	*efc-*	elec·tron·ics	*elncs*

ele·ment	*elm*	em·pha·size	*fsz*
ele·men·tary	*elmre*	em·ploy	*p*
ele·ments	*elms*	em·ployed	*p-*
ele·va·tion	*elvy*	em·ployee	*pe*
ele·va·tor	*elvar*	em·ploy·ees	*pes*
ele·va·tors	*elvars*	em·ployer	*pr*
eli·gi·bil·ity	*elʃˡ*	em·ploy·ers	*prs*
eli·gi·ble	*elʃ*	em·ploy·ing	*p-*
elimi·nate	*elma*	em·ploy·ment	*pm*
elimi·nated	*elma-*	em·ploys	*ps*
elimi·nates	*elmas*	empty	*le*
elimi·nat·ing	*elma_*	en·able	*nʃ*
elimi·na·tion	*elmy*	en·abled	*nʃ-*
else	*els*	en·ables	*nʃs*
else·where	*els r*	en·abling	*nʃ_*
em·bank·ment	*bqm*	enact	*nac*
em·bar·rass·ment	*brsm*	en·acted	*nac-*
em·bassy	*bse*	enamel	*en l*
em·blem	*bl*	en·close	*enc*
emer·gen·cies	*e rʃNes*	en·closed	*enc-*
emer·gency	*e rʃNe*	en·closes	*encs*
emo·tional	*e yl*	en·clos·ing	*enc_*
em·pha·sis	*fss*	en·clo·sure	*enc*

Word	Shorthand	Word	Shorthand
en·clo·sures	*encs*	en·forced	*nfs-*
en·code	*ncd*	en·force·ment	*nfsm*
en·cod·ing	*ncd*	en·forces	*nfss*
en·com·pass·ing	*nkps*	en·forc·ing	*nfs*
en·coun·ter	*nkr*	en·gage	*ngj*
en·coun·tered	*nkr-*	en·gaged	*ngj-*
en·cour·age	*ncrj*	en·gage·ment	*ngjm*
en·cour·aged	*ncrj-*	en·gine	*njn*
en·cour·age·ment	*ncrjm*	en·gi·neer	*njnr*
en·cour·ag·ing	*ncrj*	en·gi·neer·ing	*njnr*
en·cy·clo·pe·dia	*nsclpda*	en·gi·neers	*njnrs*
end	*n*	en·gines	*njns*
en·deavor	*ndvr*	enjoy	*njy*
en·deav·or·ing	*ndvr*	en·joy·able	*njyb*
ended	*n-*	en·joyed	*njy-*
end·ing	*n*	en·joy·ing	*njy*
en·dorse	*ndrs*	en·joy·ment	*njym*
en·dorsed	*ndrs-*	en·joys	*njys*
en·dorse·ment	*ndrsm*	en·larged	*nlrj-*
en·dorse·ments	*ndrsms*	enough	*enf*
en·dow·ment	*ndom*	en·roll	*nrl*
en·ergy	*nrje*	en·rolled	*nrl-*
en·force	*nfs*	en·roll·ment	*nrlm*

Word	Shorthand	Word	Shorthand
en·tail	*ntl*	equal·iza·tion	*eqlz*
enter	*N*	equally	*eqll*
en·tered	*N-*	equals	*eqls*
en·ter·ing	*N*	equip	*eqp*
en·ter·prise	*Nprz*	equip·ment	*eqpm*
en·ter·tain	*Ntn*	equipped	*eqp-*
en·ter·tained	*Ntn-*	eq·ui·ta·ble	*eqlB*
en·ter·tainer	*Ntnr*	eq·uity	*eqte*
en·ter·tain·ing	*Ntn*	equiva·lent	*eqvlN*
en·ter·tain·ment	*Ntnm*	era	*era*
en·thu·si·asm	*ntzez*	erect	*erc*
en·thu·si·as·tic	*ntzesc*	error	*err*
en·thu·si·as·ti·cally	*ntzescl*	er·rors	*errs*
en·tire	*ntr*	es·crow	*escro*
en·tirely	*ntrl*	es·pe·cially	*esp*
en·ti·tled	*ntll-*	es·sence	*esN*
en·trance	*NrN*	es·sen·tial	*esnsl*
en·tries	*Nres*	es·sen·tially	*esnsll*
entry	*Nre*	es·tab·lish	*esl*
en·ve·lope	*env*	es·tab·lished	*esl-*
en·ve·lopes	*envs*	es·tab·lishes	*esls*
en·vi·ron·ment	*nvrnm*	es·tab·lish·ing	*esl*
equal	*eql*	es·tab·lish·ment	*eslm*

es·tab·lish·ments	*eslms*	every	*E*
es·tate	*eSa*	eve·ry·body	*Ebde*
es·ti·mate	*eSa eSN*	eve·ry·day	*Ed*
es·ti·mated	*eSa-*	eve·ry·one	*E1*
es·ti·mates	*eSas eSNs*	eve·ry·thing	*E*
es·ti·mat·ing	*eSa*	eve·ry·where	*Er*
et cet·era	*elc*	evi·dence	*evdN*
eth·ics	*elcs*	evi·denced	*evdN-*
evalu·ate	*evla*	evi·dent	*evdN*
evalu·ated	*evla-*	evi·dently	*evdNl*
evalu·at·ing	*evla*	exact	*vc*
evalu·ation	*evluy*	ex·actly	*vcl*
even	*evn*	exam	*ᴗ*
eve·ning	*evn*	ex·ami·na·tion	*vmy*
evenly	*evnl*	ex·ami·na·tions	*vmys*
event	*evN*	ex·am·ine	*vm*
events	*evNs*	ex·am·ined	*vm-*
even·tu·ally	*evnCull*	ex·am·iner	*vmr*
ever	*E*	ex·am·in·ers	*vmrs*
ev·er·green	*Egrn*	ex·am·in·ing	*vm*
ev·er·last·ing	*ElS*	ex·am·ple	*ex*
ev·er·last·ingly	*ElSl*	ex·am·ples	*exs*
ev·er·more	*E*	exams	*ᴗs*

Word	Outline	Word	Outline
ex·ceed		ex·cuse	
ex·ceeded		exe·cute	
ex·ceed·ing		exe·cuted	
ex·ceed·ingly		exe·cu·tion	
ex·ceeds		ex·ecu·tive	
ex·cel·lent		ex·ecu·tives	
ex·cept		ex·empt	
ex·cepted		ex·emp·tion	
ex·cep·tion		ex·emp·tions	
ex·cep·tional		ex·er·cise	
ex·cep·tion·ally		ex·er·cises	
ex·cep·tions		ex·haust	
ex·cess		ex·hibit	
ex·ces·sive		ex·hib·its	
ex·change		exist	
ex·cise		ex·isted	
ex·cite		ex·is·tence	
ex·cite·ment		ex·ist·ing	
ex·cit·ing		ex·ists	
ex·cluded		ex·pand	
ex·clud·ing		ex·panded	
ex·clu·sive		ex·pand·ing	
ex·clu·sively		ex·pan·sion	

ex·pect	_vpc_	ex·plained	_vpln-_
ex·pected	_vpc-_	ex·plain·ing	_vpln_
ex·pect·ing	_vpc_	ex·plains	_vplns_
ex·pects	_vpcs_	ex·pla·na·tion	_vplny_
ex·pe·dite	_vpdi_	ex·pla·na·tions	_vplnys_
ex·pen·di·tures	_vpNCrs_	ex·plo·ra·tion	_vplry_
ex·pense	_vpN_	ex·plora·tory	_vplrlre_
ex·penses	_vpNs_	ex·plore	_vplr_
ex·pen·sive	_vpNv_	ex·plored	_vplr-_
ex·pe·ri·ence	_vp_	ex·plo·sion	_vply_
ex·pe·ri·enced	_vp-_	ex·port	_vpl_
ex·pe·ri·ences	_vps_	ex·ported	_vpl-_
ex·pe·ri·enc·ing	_vp_	ex·port·ing	_vpl_
ex·peri·ment	_vprm_	ex·ports	_vpls_
ex·peri·men·tal	_vprml_	ex·pose	_vpz_
ex·peri·ments	_vprms_	ex·posed	_vpz-_
ex·pert	_vprl_	ex·po·sure	_vpzr_
ex·perts	_vprls_	ex·po·sures	_vpzrs_
ex·pi·ra·tion	_vpry_	ex·press	_vprs_
ex·pire	_vpr_	ex·pressed	_vprs-_
ex·pired	_vpr-_	ex·press·ing	_vprs_
ex·pires	_vprs_	ex·pres·sion	_vpry_
ex·plain	_vpln_	ex·tend	_vN_

ex·tend·ed	*үn-*	faces	*fss*
ex·tend·ing	*үn_*	fac·ets	*fsts*
ex·ten·sion	*үnj*	fa·cili·tate	*fslla*
ex·ten·sive	*үnv*	fa·cil·ities	*fsl's*
ex·ten·sive·ly	*үnvl*	fa·cil·ity	*fsl'*
ex·tent	*үn*	fac·ing	*fs_*
ex·te·rior	*ɣres*	fact	*fc*
ex·ter·nal	*ɣrnl*	fac·tor	*fcr*
extra	*X*	fac·to·ries	*fctres*
ex·traor·di·nary	*Xord*	fac·tors	*fcrs*
ex·tra·sen·sory	*Xsnre*	fac·tory	*fctre*
ex·treme	*X‿*	facts	*fcs*
ex·treme·ly	*X‿l*	fac·tual	*fccul*
ex·tru·sion	*Xy*	fac·ulty	*fclle*
eye	*ι*	Fahrenheit	*frnhi*
		fail	*fl*
		failed	*fl-*
F		fail·ure	*flr*
		fair	*fr*
		fairly	*frl*
fab·ric	*fbrc*	fair·ness	*fr'*
fab·ri·ca·tion	*fbrcy*	faith	*fl*
fab·rics	*fbrcs*	faith·fully	*flfl*
face	*fs*		
faced	*fs-*		

fall	_ff_	fault	_fll_
falls	_fls_	favor	_fvr_
fa·mil·iar	_fmlr_	fa·vor·able	_fvrB_
fa·mil·iar·ize	_fmlrz_	fa·vor·ably	_fvrB_
fami·lies	_fmls_	fa·vored	_fvr-_
family	_fml_	fa·vor·ite	_fvrl_
fa·mous	_fms_	fear	_fr_
fan	_fn_	fea·si·bil·ity	_fzBl_
fancy	_fne_	fea·si·ble	_fzB_
far	_fr_	fea·ture	_fCr_
fare	_fr_	fea·tures	_fCrs_
fares	_frs_	fed·eral	_fed_
farm	_frm_	fed·er·al·ist	_fedS_
farmer	_frmr_	fed·er·al·ize	_fedz_
farm·ers	_frmrs_	fed·er·ally	_fedl_
farms	_frms_	fed·era·tion	_fdrj_
fas·ci·nat·ing	_fsna_	fee	_fe_
fash·ion	_fj_	feed	_fd_
fash·ions	_fjs_	feed·ing	_fd-_
fast	_fS_	feel	_fl_
faster	_fSr_	feel·ing	_fl-_
fat	_ft_	feel·ings	_fl=_
fa·ther	_ftr_	feels	_fls_

fees	*fes*	files	*fls*
feet	*ft*	fil·ing	*fl*
fell	*fl*	fill	*fl*
fel·low	*flo*	filled	*fl-*
fel·low·ship	*flos*	fill·ing	*fl*
felt	*fll*	fills	*fls*
fe·male	*fml*	film	*flm*
fence	*fn*	films	*flms*
fer·til·izer	*frtlzr*	fil·ters	*fltrs*
fes·ti·val	*fSvl*	final	*fnl*
few	*fu*	fi·nally	*fnll*
fewer	*fur*	fi·nance	*fnn*
fiber	*fbr*	fi·nanced	*fnn-*
fic·tion	*fcy*	fi·nan·cial	*fnnsl*
fi·del·ity	*fdlʲ*	fi·nanc·ing	*fnn*
field	*fld*	find	*fn*
fields	*flds*	find·ing	*fn*
fig·ure	*fgr*	find·ings	*fn*
fig·ured	*fgr-*	finds	*fns*
fig·ures	*fgrs*	fine	*fn*
fig·ur·ing	*fgr*	finer	*fnr*
file	*fl*	fin·est	*fnS*
filed	*fl-*	fin·ish	*fns*

fin·ished	*fns-*	flags	*flgs*
fin·ish·ing	*fns*	flame	*fl*
fire	*fr*	flam·ma·ble	*flB*
fires	*frs*	flat	*fll*
fir·ing	*fr*	flat·tered	*fldr-*
firm	*fr*	fla·vor	*flvr*
firmer	*frr*	fla·vors	*flvrs*
firm·est	*frS*	fleet	*fle*
firmly	*frl*	flex·ibil·ity	*flxB*
firm·ness	*fr'*	flight	*flu*
firms	*frs*	flights	*flis*
first	*frS 1S*	flood	*fld*
fis·cal	*fscl*	floor	*flr*
fish	*fs*	floors	*flrs*
fish·er·ies	*fsres*	flour	*flor*
fish·er·men	*fsrm*	flow	*flo*
fish·ery	*fsre*	flows	*flos*
fish·ing	*fs*	fluid	*flud*
fit	*fl*	fly	*flu*
fits	*fls*	fly·ing	*flu*
fixed	*fx-*	focus	*fcs*
fix·ture	*fxCr*	folder	*fldr*
fix·tures	*fxCrs*	fold·ers	*fldrs*

fold·ing	*fld*	fore·close	*fclz*
folks	*fcs*	forego	*fg*
fol·low	*flo*	fore·go·ing	*fg-*
fol·lowed	*flo-*	for·eign	*fn*
fol·low·ing	*flo*	fore·man	*fm*
fol·lows	*flos*	fore·men	*fm*
food	*fd*	fore·most	*fs*
foods	*fds*	fore·sight	*fsi*
foot	*ft*	for·est	*fs*
foot·age	*ftg*	for·estry	*fsre*
foot·ball	*ftbl*	for·ests	*fss*
foot·wear	*ftr*	for·ever	*fE*
for	*f*	forge	*fj*
for·bid	*fbd*	for·get	*fgt*
for·bid·den	*fbdn*	for·get·ful	*fgtf*
for·bid·ding	*fbd*	for·get·ting	*fgt*
for·bids	*fbds*	forg·ing	*fj-*
force	*fs*	for·give	*fgv*
forced	*fs-*	for·given	*fgvn*
forces	*fss*	for·give·ness	*fgv'*
forc·ing	*fs*	for·giv·ing	*fgv*
fore·cast	*fcs*	for·got	*fgt*
fore·casts	*fcss*	for·got·ten	*fgtn*

fork·lift	*fclft*	for·warded	*fw-*
form	*f*	for·ward·ing	*fw*
for·mal	*fl*	found	*fon*
for·mally	*fll*	foun·da·tion	*fony*
for·mat	*fl*	founded	*fon-*
for·ma·tion	*fy*	frac·tion	*frcy*
formed	*f-*	frame	*fr*
former	*fr*	frame·work	*fro*
for·merly	*frl*	fram·ing	*fr-*
form·ing	*f-*	fran·chise	*frncz*
forms	*fs*	fran·chises	*frnczs*
for·mula	*fla*	frank	*frq*
for·mu·late	*fla*	frankly	*frql*
for·mu·lated	*fla-*	free	*fre*
for·mu·la·tion	*fly*	free·dom	*fred*
fort	*fl*	freely	*frel*
forth	*fl*	freeze	*frz*
forth·com·ing	*flk*	freight	*fra*
for·tu·nate	*fCnl*	fre·quency	*frqne*
for·tu·nately	*fCnll*	fre·quent	*frqn*
for·tune	*fCn*	fre·quently	*frqnl*
forum	*f*	fresh	*frs*
for·ward	*fw*	friend	*frn*

friendly	_frNl_	fun·da·men·tal	_fMml_
friends	_frNs_	fun·da·men·tals	_fMmls_
friend·ship	_frNs_	funded	_fM-_
fringe	_frny_	fund·ing	_fM_
from	_fr_	funds	_fMs_
front	_frN_	funny	_fne_
frost·ing	_frS_	fur·nace	_frns_
frosty	_frSe_	fur·nish	_frns_
fro·zen	_frzn_	fur·nished	_frns-_
fuel	_ful_	fur·nishes	_frnss_
ful·fill	_ffl_	fur·nish·ing	_frns_
ful·filled	_ffl-_	fur·nish·ings	_frns_
ful·fill·ing	_ffl_	fur·ni·ture	_frnCr_
ful·fill·ment	_fflm_	fur·ther	_frlr_
full	_f_	fur·ther·more	_frlr_
fuller	_fr_	fuse	_fz_
full·est	_fS_	fus·ing	_fz-_
full·ness	_f'_	fu·ture	_fCr_
fully	_fl_		
fun	_fn_		
func·tion	_fqs_		
func·tions	_fqss_		
fund	_fN_	gain	_gn_
		gained	_gn-_

G

gains	*gns*	gen·er·al·ized	*jnz-*
gal·ley	*gle*	gen·er·al·izes	*jnzs*
gal·lon	*gln*	gen·er·al·iz·ing	*jnz-*
gal·lons	*glns*	gen·er·ally	*jnl*
gal·va·nized	*glvnz-*	gen·er·ated	*jnra-*
game	*g*	gen·er·ous	*jnrs*
games	*gs*	ge·net·ics	*jnlcs*
gap	*gp*	gen·tle·man	*jNlm*
ga·rage	*gry*	gen·tle·men	*jNlm*
gas	*gs*	genu·ine	*jnun*
gaso·line	*gsln*	get	*gt*
gate	*ga*	gets	*gts*
gath·er·ing	*glr*	get·ting	*gt*
gauge	*gj*	giant	*jiN*
gave	*gv*	gift	*gft*
gear	*gr*	gifts	*gfts*
geared	*gr-*	girl	*grl*
gen·eral	*jn*	girl·hood	*grlh*
gen·er·al·ist	*jns*	girls	*grls*
gen·er·al·ity	*jn*	give	*gv*
gen·er·al·iza·tion	*jnzj*	given	*gvn*
gen·er·al·iza·tions	*jnzjs*	gives	*gvs*
gen·er·al·ize	*jnz*	giv·ing	*gv-*

glad	*gld*	gov·ern·ing	*gvrn_*
gladly	*gldl*	gov·ern·ment	*gvt*
glands	*glNs*	gov·ern·mental	*gvtl*
glass	*gls*	gov·ern·ments	*gvts*
globe	*glb*	gov·er·nor	*gvrnr*
gloss	*gls*	gov·er·nors	*gvrnrs*
glossy	*glse*	grade	*grd*
go	*g*	grades	*grds*
goal	*gl*	gradu·ate	*grja* (v.) *grjul* (adj. or N.)
goals	*gls*	gradu·ated	*grja-*
goes	*gs*	gradu·ates	*grjas* (v.) *grjuls* (N.)
going	*g_*	gradu·at·ing	*grja_*
gold	*gld*	gradu·ation	*grjuy*
golden	*gldn*	grain	*grn*
golf	*glf*	grand	*grN*
gone	*gn*	grant	*grN*
good	*g.*	granted	*grN-*
goodly	*gl.*	grant·ing	*grN_*
good·ness	*g'*	grants	*grNs*
goods	*gs*	graph·ite	*grfi*
good·will	*gl*	grass	*grs*
got	*gl*	grate	*gr*
gov·ern	*gvrn*	grate·ful	*grf*

grate·fully	*grfl*	grow·ing	*gro_*
grati·fy·ing	*grlf_*	grown	*grn*
grati·tude	*grlld*	growth	*grl*
gray	*gra*	guar·an·tee	*grnte*
graz·ing	*grz_*	guar·an·teed	*grnte-*
great	*gr*	guar·an·tee·ing	*grnte_*
greater	*grr*	guar·an·tees	*grntes*
great·est	*grs*	guard	*grd*
greatly	*grl*	guardian	*grden*
great·ness	*gr'*	guess	*gs*
green	*grn*	guest	*gs*
greet·ings	*gre_*	guests	*gss*
gro·cery	*grsre*	gui·dance	*gdn*
gross	*grs*	guide	*gd*
ground	*gron*	guided	*gd-*
grounds	*grons*	guide·lines	*gdlns*
group	*grp*	gulf	*glf*
groups	*grps*	gun	*gn*
grove	*grv*	gym·na·sium	*jmze*
groves	*grvs*	gyp·sum	*jps*
grow	*gro*		
grower	*gror*		
grow·ers	*grors*		

H

habit	*hbt*	hap·pen	*hpn*
habi·tat	*hbtt*	hap·pened	*hpn-*
hab·its	*hbts*	hap·pen·ing	*hpn̠*
had	*h*	hap·pens	*hpns*
hadn't	*hM*	hap·pi·ness	*hpe´*
hair	*hr*	happy	*hpe*
half	*hf*	hard	*hrd*
hall	*hl*	hard·ship	*hrds*
ham·mer	*hr*	hard·ware	*hrd*
ham·mers	*hrs*	har·vest	*hrvs*
hand	*hM*	has	*hs*
hand·book	*hMbc*	hasn't	*hsM*
handi·cap	*hMcp*	hate	*ha*
handi·capped	*hMcp-*	have	*v*
han·dle	*hMl*	haven't	*vM*
han·dled	*hMl-*	hav·ing	*v̠*
han·dles	*hMls*	haz·ard	*hzrd*
han·dling	*hMl*	haz·ards	*hzrds*
hands	*hMs̄*	he	*h*
hand·some	*hM*	he's	*h's*
handy	*hMe*	head	*hd*
		head·ache	*hdac*
		headed	*hd-*

head·ing	*hd*	help	*hlp*
head·quar·ters	*hdqlrs*	helped	*hlp-*
heads	*hds*	help·ful	*hlpf*
health	*hll*	help·ing	*hlp_*
healthy	*hlle*	helps	*hlps*
hear	*hr*	hemi·sphere	*h͜sfr*
heard	*hrd*	hence	*hℳ*
hear·ing	*hr_*	her	*hr*
hear·ings	*hr=*	herb	*erb*
heart	*hrl*	here	*hr*
hearty	*hrle*	here's	*hrs*
heat	*he*	here·af·ter	*hraf*
heater	*her*	hereby	*hrb*
heat·ing	*he_*	herein	*hrn*
heavier	*hver*	hereof	*hrv*
heavily	*hvl*	hereto	*hrl*
heavy	*hve*	here·to·fore	*hrlf*
hedge	*hy*	here·un·der	*hrll*
heeded	*hd-*	here·with	*hr*
height	*hi*	heri·tage	*hrly*
heirs	*ars*	hers	*hrs*
held	*hld*	her·self	*hrsf*
hello	*hlo*	hesi·tate	*hzla*

Word	Outline	Word	Outline
high	_hi_	hold·ing	_hld_
higher	_hir_	hold·ings	_hld_
high·est	_his_	holds	_hlds_
high·lights	_hilis_	hole	_hl_
highly	_hil_	holes	_hls_
high·way	_hi a_	holi·day	_hld_
hill	_hl_	holi·days	_hlds_
hills	_hls_	home	_h_
him	_h_	home·own·ers	_h ors_
him·self	_hsf_	homes	_h s_
hire	_hr_	honor	_onr_
hired	_hr-_	hon·or·able	_onrß_
hir·ing	_hr_	hon·ored	_onr-_
his	_,_	hook	_hc_
his·to·ri·ans	_hSrens_	hoot	_hu_
his·tor·ical	_hSrcl_	hope	_hp_
his·to·ries	_hSres_	hoped	_hp-_
his·tory	_hSre_	hope·ful	_hpf_
hit	_hl_	hope·fully	_hpfl_
hobby	_hbe_	hope·less	_hpls_
hold	_hld_	hope·lessly	_hplsl_
holder	_hldr_	hopes	_hps_
hold·ers	_hldrs_	hop·ing	_hp_

ho·ri·zon	*hrzn*	hous·ing	*hoz-*	
ho·ri·zons	*hrzns*	how	*ho*	
hose	*hz*	how·ever	*hoE*	
hos·pi·tal	*hsp*	human	*hm*	
hos·pi·tal·ity	*hspll*	hum·ble	*h B*	
hos·pi·tal·iza·tion	*hspzf*	hun·dred	*H*	
hos·pi·tal·ize	*hspz*	hun·dreds	*Hs*	
hos·pi·tal·ized	*hspz-*	hun·dredth	*HL*	
hos·pi·tal·izes	*hspzs*	hurry	*hre*	
hos·pi·tal·iz·ing	*hspz_*	hurt	*hrl*	
hos·pi·tals	*hsps*	hus·band	*hzbN*	
host	*hs*	hy·drant	*hdrN*	
hot	*hl*	hy·drau·lic	*hdrlc*	
hotel	*hll*	hy·dro·elec·tric	*hdrelc*	
ho·tels	*hlls*	hy·giene	*hyn*	
hour	*hr*			
hour·glass	*hrgls*			
hourly	*hrl*	**I**		
hours	*hrs*	I	*ι*	
house	*hŏs hŏz*	I'd	*id*	
house·hold	*hoshld*	I'll	*il*	
house·keep·ing	*hoscp-*	I'm	*im*	
houses	*hoss*	I've	*iv*	

ice	_is_	im·pact	_pc_
idea	_ida_	im·part	_pt_
ideal	_idl_	im·parted	_pt-_
ideas	_idas_	im·part·ing	_pt_
iden·ti·cal	_idNcl_	im·parts	_pts_
iden·ti·fi·ca·tion	_idNff_	im·pa·tient	_psN_
iden·ti·fied	_idNf-_	im·pera·tive	_prv_
iden·tify	_idNf_	im·ple·ment	_plm_
iden·ti·fy·ing	_idNf-_	im·ple·men·ta·tion	_plmy_
if	_if_	im·ple·mented	_plm-_
ill	_il_	im·ple·ment·ing	_plm_
ill·ness	_il'_	im·port	_pt_
il·lus·trate	_ilSra_	im·por·tance	_pt_
il·lus·trated	_ilSra-_	im·por·tant	_pt_
il·lus·trat·ing	_ilSra_	im·por·tantly	_ptl_
il·lus·tra·tion	_ilSry_	im·ported	_pt-_
il·lus·tra·tions	_ilSrys_	im·port·ing	_pt_
image	_y_	im·ports	_pts_
im·agi·na·tion	_yny_	im·pose	_pz_
im·ag·ine	_yn_	im·posed	_pz-_
im·me·di·ate	‿‿	im·po·si·tion	_pzy_
im·me·di·ately	‿‿l	im·pos·si·ble	_psB_
im·me·di·ate·ness	‿‿'	im·press	_prs_

Word	Shorthand	Word	Shorthand
im·pressed	*prs-*	in·clem·ent	*nclm*
im·pres·sion	*prj*	in·clined	*ncln-*
im·pres·sive	*prsv*	in·clude	*l*
im·printed	*prM-*	in·cluded	*l-*
im·proper	*Lpr*	in·cludes	*ls*
im·prove	*pv*	in·clud·ing	*l*
im·proved	*pv-*	in·clu·sion	*lj*
im·prove·ment	*pvm*	in·clu·sive	*lsv*
im·prove·ments	*pvms*	in·come	*nk*
im·proves	*pvs*	in·com·plete	*nkp*
im·prov·ing	*pv-*	in·con·ven·ience	*nkv*
in	*n*	in·con·ven·ienced	*nkv-*
in·abil·ity	*nBl*	in·con·ven·iences	*nkvs*
in·ad·ver·tently	*nAvrlNl*	in·con·ven·ienc·ing	*nkv-*
in·as·much	*nz C*	in·con·ven·ient	*nkv*
in·cep·tion	*nspj*	in·cor·po·rate	*nc*
inch	*n*	in·cor·po·rated	*nc*
inched	*n-*	in·cor·po·rates	*ncs*
inches	*ns*	in·cor·po·rat·ing	*nc*
inch·ing	*n*	in·cor·po·ra·tion	*ncj*
in·ci·dent	*ndN*	in·cor·po·ra·tions	*ncjs*
in·ci·den·tal	*ndNl*	in·cor·rect	*ncrc*
in·ci·den·tally	*ndNll*	in·crease	*ncrs*

in·creased	*ncrs-*	in·di·rect	*ndr*
in·creases	*ncrss*	in·di·rectly	*ndrl*
in·creas·ing	*ncrs*	in·di·vidual	*Nv*
in·creas·ingly	*ncrsf*	in·di·vidu·al·ist	*NvS*
in·cre·ments	*ncrms*	in·di·vidu·al·ity	*Nvᴸ*
in·cu·ba·tor	*ncbar*	in·di·vidu·ally	*Nvl*
in·cu·ba·tors	*ncbars*	in·di·vidu·als	*Nvs*
in·curred	*ncr-*	in·dulge	*ndlj*
in·debted	*ndl-*	in·dus·trial	*Nl*
in·debt·ed·ness	*ndl-'*	in·dus·tri·al·ism	*Nlz*
in·deed	*ndd*	in·dus·tri·al·ist	*NlS*
in·dem·nity	*nd_nle*	in·dus·tri·al·iza·tion	*Nlzj*
in·de·pend·ence	*NpNN*	in·dus·tri·al·ize	*Nlz*
in·de·pend·ent	*NpNN*	in·dus·tri·al·izes	*Nlzs*
index	*Nx*	in·dus·tri·ally	*Nll*
in·di·cate	*Nca*	in·dus·tries	*Ns*
in·di·cated	*Nca-*	in·dus·tri·ous	*Ns*
in·di·cates	*Ncas*	in·dus·tri·ously	*Nsl*
in·di·cat·ing	*Nca*	in·dus·tri·ous·ness	*Ns'*
in·di·ca·tion	*Ncj*	in·dus·try	*N*
in·dif·fer·ent	*ndfrN*	in·evi·ta·ble	*nevlB*
in·di·gent	*NjN*	in·evi·ta·bly	*nevlB*
in·dig·nant	*ndgnN*	in·ex·pen·sive	*nxpNv*

Word	Shorthand	Word	Shorthand
in·ex·pe·ri·ence	*nxp*	in·jured	*njr-*
in·ex·pe·ri·enced	*nxp-*	in·ju·ries	*njres*
in·fir·mary	*nfrre*	in·jury	*njre*
in·fla·tion	*nfly*	ink	*iq*
in·fla·tion·ary	*nflyre*	inks	*iqs*
in·flu·ence	*nfluN*	in·land	*nlN*
in·flu·en·tial	*nflunsl*	in·mate	*n a*
in·form	*nf*	in·mates	*n as*
in·for·mal	*nfl*	inn	*n*
in·for·ma·tion	*inf*	inner	*nr*
in·for·ma·tional	*infl*	in·no·va·tion	*nvy*
in·forma·tive	*nf v*	in·op·era·tive	*nopv*
in·formed	*nf -*	input	*npl*
in·form·ing	*nf*	in·quire	*nq*
in·forms	*nf s*	in·quired	*nq-*
in·habi·tants	*nhblNs*	in·quir·ies	*nqes*
in·heri·tance	*nhrlN*	in·quir·ing	*nq_*
ini·tial	*insl*	in·quiry	*nqe*
ini·tially	*insll*	in·sert	*nsrl*
ini·ti·ate	*insa insel*	in·serted	*nsrl-*
ini·ti·ated	*insa-*	in·ser·tion	*nsry*
ini·tia·tion	*insey*	in·serts	*nsrls*
in·jec·tion	*njcy*	in·side	*nsd*

in·sight	*nsi*	in·struct	*nSrc*
in·sist	*nsS*	in·structed	*nSrc-*
in·so·far	*nsofr*	in·struc·tion	*nSrcy*
in·spect	*nspc*	in·struc·tional	*nSrcyl*
in·spected	*nspc-*	in·struc·tions	*nSrcys*
in·spec·tion	*nspcy*	in·struc·tor	*nSrcr*
in·spec·tors	*nspcrs*	in·struc·tors	*nSrcrs*
in·spi·ra·tion	*nspry*	in·stru·ment	*nSrm*
in·stall	*nSl*	in·stru·ments	*nSrms*
in·stal·la·tion	*nSly*	in·suf·fi·cient	*nsfsN*
in·stal·la·tions	*nSlys*	in·sur·abil·ity	*nsrBl*
in·stalled	*nSl-*	in·sur·able	*nsrB*
in·stall·ing	*nSl̲*	in·sur·ance	*ins*
in·stall·ment	*nSlm*	in·sure	*nsr*
in·stall·ments	*nSlms*	in·sured	*nsr-*
in·stance	*nSN*	in·sur·ing	*nsr̲*
in·stances	*nSNs*	in·teg·rity	*nlgrle*
in·stant	*nSN*	in·tel·lec·tual	*NlcCul*
in·stead	*nSd*	in·tel·li·gence	*nllyN*
in·sti·tute	*nSlu*	in·tel·li·gent	*nllyN*
in·sti·tu·tion	*nSly*	in·tend	*nlN*
in·sti·tu·tional	*nSlyl*	in·tended	*nlN-*
in·sti·tu·tions	*nSlys*	in·tense	*nlN*

in·ten·sive		into	
in·tent		in·toxi·cants	
in·ten·tion		in·tra·mu·ral	
in·ter·change		in·trigu·ing	
in·ter·est		in·tro·duce	
in·ter·ested		in·tro·duced	
in·ter·est·ing		in·tro·duc·ing	
in·ter·ests		in·tro·duc·tion	
in·ter·fere		in·tro·duc·tory	
in·terim		in·valu·able	
in·te·rior		in·ven·tion	
in·ter·me·di·ate		in·ven·to·ries	
in·ter·nal		in·ven·tory	
in·ter·na·tional		in·vest	
in·ter·pret		in·vested	
in·ter·pre·ta·tion		in·ves·ti·gate	
in·ter·state		in·ves·ti·gated	
in·ter·val		in·ves·ti·gat·ing	
in·ter·vals		in·ves·ti·ga·tion	
in·ter·ven·ing		in·ves·ti·ga·tions	
in·ter·view		in·vest·ment	
in·ter·view·ing		in·vest·ments	
in·ter·views		in·ves·tors	

Word	Outline	Word	Outline
in·vi·ta·tion		is·sues	
in·vite		is·su·ing	
in·vited		it	
in·vit·ing		it's	
in·voice		item	
in·voiced		item·ized	
in·voices		items	
in·voic·ing		its	
in·volve		it·self	
in·volved		ivory	
in·volve·ment			
in·volves			
in·volv·ing			

J

Word	Outline	Word	Outline
iron		jacket	
irons		jani·tor	
ir·regu·lar		jet	
ir·ri·ga·tion		jew·elry	
is		jew·els	
is·land		job	
isn't		job·ber	
is·su·ance		jobs	
issue		join	
is·sued		joined	

join·ing	*jyn_*
joins	*jyns*
joint	*jyN*
jointly	*jyNl*
jour·nal	*jrnl*
judge	*jj*
judges	*jjs*
judg·ment	*jjm*
judg·ments	*jjms*
ju·di·ci·ary	*jdsere*
jun·ior	*jr*
jun·iors	*jrs*
jur·is·dic·tion	*jrsdcy*
jury	*jre*
just	*js*
jus·tice	*jss*
jus·ti·fi·ca·tion	*jsfj*
jus·ti·fied	*jsf-*
jus·tify	*jsf*
ju·ve·nile	*jvnl*

K

keen	*cn*
keep	*cp*
keep·ing	*cp_*
keeps	*cps*
kept	*cpl*
key	*ce*
key·board	*cebrd*
key punch	*cepnC*
keys	*ces*
kill	*cl*
killed	*cl-*
kind	*cN*
kind·est	*cNs*
kindly	*cNl*
kinds	*cNs*
kit	*cl*
kitchen	*cCn*
kits	*cls*
knew	*nu*
know	*no*
know·ing	*no_*

knowl·edge	*nlg*	land·own·ers	*lNors*
known	*nn*	lands	*lNs*
knows	*nos*	lane	*ln*
		lanes	*lns*

L

		lan·guage	*lgy*
		lapse	*lps*
label	*lB*	lapsed	*lps-*
la·beled	*lB-*	large	*lg*
la·bel·ing	*lB̲*	largely	*lgl*
la·bels	*lBs*	larger	*lgr*
labor	*lbr*	larg·est	*lgs*
labo·ra·to·ries	*lbrlres*	last	*ls*
labo·ra·tory	*lbrlre*	late	*la*
la·bor·ers	*lbrrs*	later	*lar*
lack	*lc*	lat·est	*las*
la·dies	*ldes*	lat·ter	*llr*
lad·ing	*ld̲*	launch	*lnC*
lady	*lde*	launch·ing	*lnC̲*
lake	*lc*	launch·ings	*lnC̲̲*
lakes	*lcs*	law	*la*
lamp	*lp*	lawn	*ln*
lamps	*lps*	laws	*las*
land	*lN*	law·yer	*lar*

law·yers	*lars*	leaves	*lvs*
lay	*la*	leav·ing	*lv*
lay·out	*laol*	lec·ture	*lcCr*
lead	*ld*	led	*ld*
leader	*ldr*	ledger	*ljr*
lead·ers	*ldrs*	left	*lft*
lead·er·ship	*ldrs*	legal	*lgl*
lead·ing	*ld*	leg·is·la·tion	*ljsly*
leads	*lds*	leg·is·la·tive	*ljslv*
leaf	*lf*	leg·is·la·ture	*ljslCr*
leaf·let	*lflt*	lend	*en*
league	*lg*	lend·ing	*en*
lean·ing	*ln*	length	*lgt*
learn	*lrn*	lengths	*lgts*
learned	*lrn-*	lens	*lnz*
learn·ing	*lrn*	less	*ls*
lease	*ls*	les·son	*lsn*
leased	*ls-*	let	*ll*
leases	*lss*	let's	*ll's*
leas·ing	*ls*	lets	*lls*
least	*ls*	let·ter	*L*
leather	*llr*	let·ter·head	*Lhd*
leave	*lv*	let·ter·ing	*L*

let·ters	*Ls*	light	*li*
let·ting	*li*	light·ing	*li*
level	*lvl*	lights	*lis*
lev·els	*lvls*	like	*lc*
li·abil·ities	*liß ls*	like·li·hood	*lclh*
li·abil·ity	*liß l*	likely	*lcl*
li·able	*liß*	like·wise	*lcz*
li·ai·son	*lezn*	lime	*l*
lib·eral	*lbrl*	limit	*lt*
lib·erty	*lbrle*	limi·ta·tion	*lty*
li·brary	*lbrre*	limi·ta·tions	*ltys*
li·cense	*lsN*	lim·ited	*lt-*
li·censed	*lsN-*	lim·its	*lts*
li·censes	*lsNs*	line	*ln*
li·cens·ing	*lsN*	lineal	*lnel*
lie	*li*	linear	*lner*
lien	*ln*	lined	*ln-*
lies	*lis*	lin·ens	*lnns*
lieu	*lu*	lines	*lns*
life	*lf*	liq·uid	*lqd*
life·time	*lft*	liq·ui·date	*lqda*
lift	*lfl*	list	*lS*
lifts	*lfls*	listed	*lS-*

lis·ten	*lsn*		lo·cal·ity	*lcl ¹*	
lis·tened	*lsn -*		lo·cally	*lcll*	
lis·ten·ing	*lsn*		lo·cate	*lca*	
list·ing	*lS*		lo·cated	*lca -*	
list·ings	*lS*		lo·ca·tion	*lcy*	
lists	*lSs*		lo·ca·tions	*lcys*	
lit·er·ally	*llrll*		lock·ers	*lcrs*	
lit·era·ture	*lil*		locks	*lcs*	
lit·tle	*lll*		lodge	*ly*	
live	*lv*		lodges	*lys*	
lived	*lv -*		log	*lg*	
lively	*lvl*		log·ical	*lycl*	
lives	*lvo*		long	*lg*	
live·stock	*lvSc*		longer	*lgr*	
liv·ing	*lv*		long·est	*lgS*	
load	*ld*		look	*lc*	
loaded	*ld -*		looked	*lc -*	
load·ing	*ld*		look·ing	*lc*	
loads	*lds*		looks	*lcs*	
loan	*ln*		loop	*lp*	
loans	*lns*		loose	*ls*	
lobby	*lbe*		lose	*lz*	
local	*lcl*		loss	*ls*	

losses	*lss*		**M**
lost	*ls*		
lot	*ll*	ma·chine	*An*
lots	*lls*	ma·chin·ery	*Anre*
lounge	*lony*	ma·chines	*Ans*
love	*lv*	mad	*d*
loved	*lv-*	made	*d*
low	*lo*	maga·zine	*gzn*
lower	*lor*	maga·zines	*gzns*
low·ered	*lor-*	magic	*jc*
low·est	*los*	mag·nifi·cent	*gnfsN*
loyal	*lyl*	mail	*l*
loy·alty	*lylle*	mailed	*l-*
lu·bri·ca·tion	*lvrcy*	mailer	*lr*
luck	*lc*	mail·ing	*l*
lucky	*lce*	mail·ings	*l*
lug·gage	*lgj*	main	*n*
lump	*l p*	mainly	*nl*
lunch	*lnC*	mains	*ns*
lunch·eon	*lnCn*	main·tain	*nln*
		main·tained	*nln-*
		main·tain·ing	*nln*
		main·tains	*nlns*

Word	Shorthand	Word	Shorthand
main·te·nance		manned	
major		man·ner	
ma·jor·ity		man·power	
ma·jors		manual	
make		manu·als	
maker		manu·fac·ture	
mak·ers		manu·fac·tured	
makes		manu·fac·turer	
mak·ing		manu·fac·tur·ers	
male		manu·fac·tures	
ma·li·cious		manu·fac·tur·ing	
man		many	
man·age		map	
man·aged		maps	
man·age·ment		mar·ginal	
man·age·ments		ma·rine	
man·ager		mark	
mana·gerial		marked	
man·ag·ers		mar·ket	
man·ages		mar·keted	
man·ag·ing		mar·ket·ing	
man·da·tory		mar·kets	
man-hours		mark·ing	

marks	_rcs_	maybe	_ab_
mar·riage	_ry_	mayor	_ar_
mar·ried	_re-_	me	_e_
marsh	_rsh_	meal	_l_
mass	_s_	meals	_ls_
mas·ter	_Sr_	mean	_m_
mas·ters	_Srs_	mean·ing	_m_
mat	_t_	mean·ing·ful	_mf_
match	_C_	means	_ms_
match·ing	_C_	meant	_m_
ma·te·rial	_trel_	mean·time	_mt_
ma·te·ri·als	_trels_	mean·while	_ml_
mathe·mat·ical	_t tcl_	meas·ure	_zr_
mathe·mat·ics	_t tcs_	meas·ured	_zr-_
mats	_ts_	meas·ure·ment	_zrm_
mat·ter	_tr_	meas·ure·ments	_zrms_
mat·ters	_trs_	meas·ures	_zrs_
mat·tress	_trs_	meat	_e_
ma·ture	_tr_	me·chan·ical	_cncl_
ma·tured	_tr-_	me·chan·ics	_cncs_
ma·tur·ity	_tr_	mecha·nism	_cnz_
maxi·mum	_xm_	mecha·nized	_cnz-_
may	_a_	media	_da_

med·ical	*dcl*	mer·can·tile	*rcntl*
medi·care	*dcr*	mer·chan·dise	*dse*
medi·cine	*dsn*	mer·chan·dises	*dses*
me·dium	*de*	mer·chan·dis·ing	*dse*
meet	*e*	mer·chant	*rCN*
meet·ing	*e*	mer·cury	*rcre*
meet·ings	*e*	mere	*r*
meets	*es*	merely	*rl*
mel·low	*lo*	merger	*rjr*
mem·ber	*mbr*	merit	*rl*
mem·bers	*mbrs*	mer·its	*rls*
mem·ber·ship	*mbrs*	merry	*re*
mem·ber·ships	*mbrss*	mes·sage	*sj*
memo	*mo*	met	*l*
memo·ran·dum	*mrN*	metal	*ll*
me·mo·rial	*rel*	me·tal·lic	*llc*
memory	*mre*	met·als	*lls*
memos	*mos*	meter	*m*
men	*m*	me·ters	*ms*
men·tal	*mll*	method	*ld*
men·tion	*my*	meth·ods	*lds*
men·tioned	*my-*	met·ro·poli·tan	*lrplln*
menu	*mu*	mid·dle	*dl*

might	⌐ı	min·utes	mls
mile	⌐l	mir·rors	rrs
mile·age	⌐ly	mis·cel·la·ne·ous	Mlnes
miles	⌐ls	mis·lay	Mla
mili·tary	⌐llre	mis·lead	Mld
milk	⌐lc	mis·place	Mpls
mill	⌐l	mis·placed	Mpls-
mil·lion	M	mis·print	MprM
mil·lion·aire	Mr	miss	m
mil·lions	Ms	missed	m-
mil·lionth	Ml	miss·ing	m̲
mills	⌐ls	mis·sion	⌐y
mind	m	mis·take	Mlc
minds	ms	mis·taken	Mlcn
mine	m	mis·un·der·stand	MUSN
min·eral	mrl	mis·un·der·stand·ing	MUSN̲
min·er·als	mrls	mis·un·der·stands	MUSN̄s
mini·mize	mz	mis·un·der·stood	MUSd
mini·mum	mm	mix	x
min·ing	m̲	mixed	x-
minor	mr	mix·ing	x̲
mi·nor·ity	mrl	mo·bile	B̲
min·ute	ml	mode	d

model	*dl*	mother	*lr*
mod·els	*dls*	mo·tion	*y*
mod·ern	*drn*	motor	*lr*
mod·est	*dS*	mo·tors	*lrs*
modi·fi·ca·tion	*df*	mount	*oN*
modi·fi·ca·tions	*dfs*	moun·tain	*oNn*
modi·fied	*df-*	mounted	*oN-*
modify	*df*	move	*v*
mo·ment	*m*	moved	*v-*
money	*me*	move·ment	*vm*
month	*o*	move·ments	*vms*
monthly	*ol*	moves	*vs*
months	*os*	movie	*ve*
moral	*rl*	mov·ies	*ves*
more	*—*	mov·ing	*v_*
more·over	*o*	Mr.	*r*
morn·ing	*rn_*	Mrs.	*rs*
mort·gage	*rgj*	Ms.	*s*
mort·ga·gee	*rgje*	much	*C*
mort·gages	*rgjs*	mud	*d*
most	*S*	mul·ti·ple	*llpl*
motel	*ll*	mu·nici·pal	*nspl*
mo·tels	*lls*	mu·seum	*ze*

music	*zc*	na·tion·als	*nyls*
mu·si·cians	*zjs*	na·tions	*nys*
must	*s*	na·tion·wide	*nyıd*
mus·ter	*Sr*	na·tive	*nv*
mu·tual	*Cul*	natu·ral	*nCrl*
mu·tu·ally	*Cull*	natu·rally	*nCrll*
my	*ı*	na·ture	*nCr*
my·self	*ısf*	navel	*nvl*
mys·te·ri·ous	*Mlres*	navy	*nve*
mys·tery	*Mlre*	near	*nr*

N

		nearby	*nrb*
		near·est	*nrs*
		nearly	*nrl*
name	*n*	nec·es·sarily	*nesl*
named	*n-*	nec·es·sary	*nes*
name·less	*nls*	ne·ces·si·tate	*nssla*
namely	*nl*	ne·ces·sity	*nssl*
names	*ns*	need	*nd*
nar·rate	*nra*	needed	*nd-*
nar·ra·tive	*nrv*	need·less	*ndls*
na·tion	*ny*	needs	*nds*
na·tional	*nyl*	nega·tive	*ngv*
na·tion·ally	*nyll*	ne·glected	*nglc-*

ne·go·ti·ate	*ngsa*	no	*no*
ne·go·ti·ated	*ngsa-*	nomi·nal	*nml*
ne·go·ti·at·ing	*ngsa*	nomi·nate	*nma*
ne·go·tia·tion	*ngsej*	nomi·nated	*nma-*
ne·go·tia·tions	*ngsejs*	nomi·na·tion	*nmy*
neigh·bor·hood	*nbrh*	nomi·na·tions	*nmys*
nei·ther	*nlr*	none	*nn*
net	*nl*	non·profit	*nnpfl*
net·work	*nlo*	noon	*nn*
neu·tral	*nlrl*	nor	*nr*
never	*nvr*	nor·mal	*nrl*
nev·er·the·less	*nvrls*	nor·mally	*nrll*
new	*nu*	north	*N*
newest	*nus*	north·east	*NE*
newly	*nul*	north·east·erly	*NErl*
news	*nz*	north·east·ern	*NErn*
news·let·ter	*nzl*	north·ern	*Nrn*
news·pa·per	*nzppr*	north·ward	*Nw*
news·pa·pers	*nzpprs*	north·west	*NW*
next	*nx*	north·west·ern	*NWrn*
nice	*ns*	nose	*nz*
night	*ni*	not	*n*
nights	*nis*	no·tary	*nlre*

no·ta·tion	*nly*	num·ber·less	*Nols*
no·ta·tions	*nlys*	num·bers	*Nos*
note	*nl*	nu·mer·ous	*n rs*
noted	*nl-*	nurse	*nrs*
notes	*nls*	nurs·ery	*nrsre*
noth·ing	*nlq*	nurses	*nrss*
no·tice	*nls*	nurs·ing	*nrs_*
no·tice·able	*nlsθ*	nut·shell	*nlsl*
no·tice·ably	*nlsθ*		
no·ticed	*nls-*		
no·tices	*nlss*		**O**
no·ti·fi·ca·tion	*nlff*		
no·ti·fied	*nlf-*	ob·ject	*obyc*
no·ti·fies	*nlfs*	ob·jec·tion	*obycy*
no·tify	*nlf*	ob·jec·tions	*obycys*
no·ti·fy·ing	*nlf_*	ob·jec·tive	*obycv*
not·with·stand·ing	*n SN*	ob·jec·tives	*obycvs*
now	*no*	ob·li·gated	*oblga-*
noz·zle	*nzl*	ob·li·ga·tion	*oblgy*
nu·clear	*ncler*	ob·li·ga·tions	*oblgys*
num·ber	*No*	oblige	*obly*
num·bered	*No-*	ob·ser·vance	*obzrvN*
num·ber·ing	*No_*	ob·ser·va·tion	*obzrvy*
		ob·ser·va·tions	*obzrvys*

Word	Shorthand	Word	Shorthand
ob·serve	*obzrv*	oc·curs	*ocrs*
ob·served	*obzrv-*	ocean	*oy*
ob·so·lete	*obsle*	odd	*od*
ob·tain	*obtn*	of	*v*
ob·tain·able	*obtnß*	off	*of*
ob·tained	*obtn-*	offer	*ofr*
ob·tain·ing	*obtn*	of·fered	*ofr-*
ob·vi·ous	*obves*	of·fer·ing	*ofr*
ob·vi·ously	*obvesl*	of·fer·ings	*ofr*
oc·ca·sion	*ocy*	of·fers	*ofrs*
oc·ca·sional	*ocyl*	of·fice	*ofs*
oc·ca·sion·ally	*ocyll*	of·fi·cer	*ofsr*
oc·ca·sions	*ocys*	of·fi·cers	*ofsrs*
oc·cu·pancy	*ocpne*	of·fices	*ofss*
oc·cu·pa·tion	*ocpy*	of·fi·cial	*ofsl*
oc·cu·pa·tional	*ocpyl*	of·fi·cially	*ofsll*
oc·cu·pa·tions	*ocpys*	of·fi·cials	*ofsls*
oc·cu·pied	*ocpi-*	off·set	*ofsl*
oc·cupy	*ocpi*	often	*ofn*
occur	*ocr*	oil	*yl*
oc·curred	*ocr-*	oils	*yls*
oc·cur·rence	*ocrn*	okay	*ok*
oc·cur·ring	*ocr*	old	*old*

older	_oldr_	op·er·at·ing	_op_
omit	_ont_	op·era·tion	_opj_
omit·ted	_ont-_	op·era·tional	_opjl_
on	_o_	op·era·tion·ally	_opjll_
once	_oN_	op·era·tions	_opjs_
on·com·ing	_ok_	op·era·tor	_opr_
on·go·ing	_og-_	op·era·tors	_oprs_
on·looker	_olcr_	opin·ion	_opn_
on·look·ing	_olc_	opin·ion·ated	_opna-_
only	_ol_	opin·ions	_opns_
on·rush	_ors_	op·por·tu·ni·ties	_opls_
onset	_osl_	op·por·tu·nity	_opl_
onto	_ol_	op·posed	_opz-_
on·ward	_ow_	op·po·si·tion	_opzj_
on·wards	_ows_	op·ti·mum	_oplm_
open	_opn_	op·tion	_opj_
opened	_opn-_	op·tional	_opjl_
open·ing	_opn_	op·tions	_opjs_
open·ings	_opn_	or	_or_
opens	_opns_	oral	_orl_
op·er·ate	_op_	or·ange	_ornj_
op·er·ated	_op-_	orbit	_orbl_
op·er·ates	_ops_	order	_od_

or·dered	*od-*	origi·nally	*orynll*
or·der·ing	*od*	origi·nals	*orynls*
or·der·lies	*odls*	origi·nate	*oryna*
or·der·li·ness	*odl'*	origi·nat·ing	*oryna*
or·derly	*odl*	or·tho·pe·dic	*orlpdc*
or·ders	*ods*	other	*ol*
or·di·nance	*ordnN*	oth·ers	*ols*
or·di·narily	*ordl*	oth·er·wise	*olz*
or·di·nary	*ord*	ought	*ol*
or·gan·iza·tion	*ogl*	ounce	*oz*
or·gan·iza·tional	*ogjl*	ounces	*ozs*
or·gan·iza·tion·ally	*ogjll*	our	*r*
or·gan·iza·tions	*ogjs*	ours	*rs*
or·gan·ize	*og*	our·selves	*rsvs*
or·gan·ized	*og-*	out	*ol*
or·gan·izer	*ogr*	outer	*olr*
or·gan·iz·ers	*ogrs*	out·fit	*olfl*
or·gan·iz·ing	*og_*	out·let	*olll*
ori·ent	*oreN*	out·lets	*ollls*
ori·en·ta·tion	*oreNy*	out·line	*olln*
ori·ented	*oreN-*	out·lined	*olln-*
ori·gin	*oryn*	out·lines	*ollns*
origi·nal	*orynl*	out·lin·ing	*olln*

out·look	_ollc_	over·throw	_Olro_
out·put	_olpl_	over·thrown	_Olrn_
out·side	_olsd_	over·time	_Ol_
out·stand·ing	_olSN_	over·weight	_Oa_
over	_O_	over·whelm	_Ol_
over·all	_Oa_	over·whelm·ing	_Ol_
over·charge	_OG_	over·whelm·ingly	_Olil_
over·come	_Ok_	over·work	_Oo_
overdo	_Odu_	owe	_o_
over·draft	_Odrfl_	owed	_o -_
over·due	_Odu_	own	_o_
over·ex·pen·di·ture	_OxpNCr_	owned	_o -_
over·head	_Ohd_	owner	_or_
over·lay	_Ola_	own·ers	_ors_
over·look	_Olc_	own·er·ship	_ors_
over·looked	_Olc-_	own·ing	_o_
overly	_Ol_	owns	_os_
over·night	_Oni_		
over·paid	_Opd_		
over·pay·ment	_Opam_	**P**	
over·rid·ing	_Ord_		
over·seas	_Oses_	pace	_ps_
over·sight	_Osi_	pack	_pc_
		pack·age	_pcj_

pack·aged	*pcj-*	pam·phlets	*p flls*
pack·ages	*pcjs*	pan	*pn*
pack·ag·ing	*pcj-*	pane	*pn*
packed	*pc-*	panel	*pnl*
pack·ers	*pcrs*	pan·els	*pnls*
pack·ets	*pcls*	paper	*ppr*
pack·ing	*pc_*	pa·pers	*pprs*
pad	*pd*	pa·per·work	*ppro*
page	*pj*	par	*pr*
pages	*pjs*	para·graph	*prgrf*
pag·ing	*pj-*	par·al·lel	*prll*
paid	*pd*	par·al·lels	*prlls*
paint	*pN*	par·cel	*prsl*
painted	*pN-*	par·cels	*prsls*
paint·ing	*pN_*	par·don	*prdn*
paint·ings	*pN=*	par·ent	*prN*
paints	*pNs*	par·ent·hood	*prNh*
pair	*pr*	par·ents	*prNs*
pairs	*prs*	par·ish	*prt*
pal·let	*pll*	park	*prc*
pal·lets	*plls*	park·ing	*prc_*
palm	*p*	parks	*prcs*
pam·phlet	*p fll*	park·way	*prca*

part	*pt*	pas·sage	*psy*
parted	*pt-*	pass·book	*psbc*
par·tial	*prsl*	passed	*ps-*
par·tici·pant	*ppN*	pas·sen·ger	*psnyr*
par·tici·pants	*ppNs*	pas·sen·gers	*psnyrs*
par·tici·pate	*pp*	passes	*pss*
par·tici·pated	*pp-*	pass·ing	*ps_*
par·tici·pates	*pps*	pass·port	*pspt*
par·tici·pat·ing	*pp_*	past	*ps*
par·tici·pa·tion	*ppy*	pas·ture	*psCr*
par·ti·cle	*ptcl*	paths	*pts*
par·ticu·lar	*ptc*	pa·tience	*psN*
par·ticu·larly	*ptcl*	pa·tient	*psN*
par·ticu·lars	*ptcs*	pa·tients	*psNs*
par·ties	*ples*	patio	*pto*
part·ing	*pt_*	pa·tron·age	*ptrny*
partly	*ptl*	pat·tern	*ptrn*
part·ner	*ptnr*	pat·terns	*ptrns*
part·ners	*ptnrs*	pav·ing	*pv_*
part·ner·ship	*ptnrs*	pay	*pa*
parts	*pts*	pay·able	*pab*
party	*pte*	pay·ing	*pa_*
pass	*ps*	pay·ment	*pam*

pay·ments	*pams*	per·form	*Pf*
pay·roll	*parl*	per·form·ance	*PfM*
pays	*pas*	per·formed	*Pf-*
peace	*ps*	per·form·ing	*Pf_*
peak	*pc*	per·haps	*Ph*
pen	*pn*	pe·riod	*pred*
pen·alty	*pnlle*	pe·ri·odic	*predc*
pen·cil	*pNl*	pe·ri·od·ically	*predcll*
pen·cils	*pNls*	pe·ri·od·icals	*predcls*
pend·ing	*pN*	pe·ri·ods	*preds*
pene·tra·tion	*pnlry*	per·ma·nent	*PmN*
pen·sion	*pny*	per·ma·nently	*PmNl*
peo·ple	*ppl*	per·mis·si·ble	*P sB*
per	*P*	per·mis·sion	*Py*
per·cent	*%*	per·mit	*Pl*
per·cent·age	*%y*	per·mits	*Pls*
per·cent·ages	*%ys*	per·mit·ted	*Pl-*
per·cen·tile	*%l*	per·mit·ting	*Pl*
per·cen·tiles	*%ls*	per·sist·ency	*PsSNe*
per·cents	*%s*	per·sist·ent	*PsSN*
per·fect	*Pfc*	per·son	*Psn*
per·fectly	*Pfcl*	per·sonal	*Psnl*
per·fo·rated	*Pfra-*	per·son·al·ities	*Psnl⁶*

per·son·al·ity	*Psnl'*	phrase	*frz*
per·son·al·ized	*Psnlz-*	phys·ical	*fzcl*
per·son·ally	*Psnll*	phys·ically	*fzcll*
per·son·nel	*Psnl*	phy·si·cian	*fzl*
per·sons	*Psns*	phy·si·cians	*fzls*
per·spec·tive	*Pspcr*	phys·ics	*fzcs*
per·tain·ing	*Pln*	piano	*peno*
per·ti·nent	*PlnN*	pick	*pc*
pe·ti·tion	*ply*	picked	*pc-*
pe·ti·tions	*plys*	pickup	*pcp*
pe·tro·leum	*plrle*	pic·ture	*pccr*
phase	*fz*	pic·tures	*pccrs*
phases	*fzs*	piece	*ps*
phi·loso·phy	*flsfe*	pieces	*pss*
phone	*fn*	pilot	*pll*
photo	*flo*	pin	*pn*
pho·to·cop·ies	*flocpes*	pine	*pn*
pho·to·copy	*flocpe*	pink	*pg*
pho·to·graph	*flogrf*	pins	*pns*
pho·to·graphic	*flogrfc*	pio·neer	*pinr*
pho·to·graphs	*flogrfs*	pipe	*pp*
pho·tos	*flos*	pipe·line	*ppln*
pho·to·stat	*flSl*	pipe·lines	*pplns*

pit·falls	*ptfls*	play	*pla*
place	*pls*	played	*pla-*
placed	*pls-*	play·ful	*plaf*
place·ment	*plsm*	play·ing	*pla̱*
place·ments	*plsms*	plays	*plas*
places	*plss*	plaza	*plza*
plac·ing	*pls̱*	pleas·ant	*plzN*
plain	*pln*	please	*p*
plain·tiff	*plNf*	pleased	*p-*
plan	*pln*	pleases	*ps*
plane	*pln*	pleas·ing	*p̱*
plane·tarium	*plntre*	pleas·ure	*plzr*
planned	*pln-*	pleas·ures	*plzrs*
plan·ning	*plṉ*	pledge	*plj*
plans	*plns*	plenty	*plNe*
plant	*plN*	plugs	*plgs*
plant·ing	*plṈ*	plumb·ing	*pḻ*
plants	*plNs*	plus	*pls*
plas·tic	*plSc*	pneu·matic	*nlc*
plas·tics	*plScs*	pocket	*pcl*
plate	*pla*	point	*py*
plates	*plas*	pointed	*py-*
plat·form	*plf*	points	*pys*

poles	*pls*	po·si·tion	*pzj*
po·lice	*pls*	po·si·tions	*pzjs*
poli·cies	*plses*	posi·tive	*pzv*
policy	*plse*	pos·ses·sion	*pzj*
poli·cy·hol·der	*plsehldr*	pos·si·bil·ities	*psß ls*
poli·cy·hol·ders	*plsehldrs*	pos·si·bil·ity	*psßl*
po·lit·ical	*pltcl*	pos·si·ble	*psß*
poli·tics	*pltcs*	pos·si·bly	*psß*
poll	*pl*	post	*pß*
pol·lu·tion	*ply*	post·age	*pßj*
pool	*pl*	postal	*pßl*
pools	*pls*	posted	*pß-*
poor	*pr*	post·ers	*pßrs*
popu·lar	*pplr*	post·man	*pß m*
popu·la·tion	*pply*	post·mark	*pß rc*
popu·la·tions	*pplys*	post·paid	*pßpd*
port	*pl*	po·ten·tial	*ptnsl*
port·able	*plß*	po·ten·tials	*ptnsls*
port·fo·lio	*plflo*	poul·try	*pltre*
port·fo·lios	*plflos*	pound	*lb*
por·tion	*pry*	pounds	*lbs*
por·tions	*prys*	pow·der	*podr*
ports	*pls*	power	*por*

pow·ered	*por-*	prepa·ra·tion	*prpry*
pow·ers	*pors*	pre·pare	*Ppr*
prac·ti·cal	*prctcl*	pre·pared	*Ppr-*
prac·ti·cally	*prctcll*	pre·par·ing	*Ppr*
prac·tice	*prcls*	pre·scribe	*PS*
prac·tices	*prclss*	pre·scribed	*PS-*
pray	*pra*	pre·scrip·tion	*PSy*
pre·ced·ing	*Psd*	pres·ence	*pryN*
pre·cious	*prss*	pre·sent (*v.*)	*p*
pre·cisely	*Pssl*	pres·ent (*n.*) *or* (*adj.*)	*p*
pre·ci·sion	*Psy*	pres·en·ta·tion	*Py*
pre·clude	*Pcld*	pres·en·ta·tions	*Pys*
pre·dict	*Pdc*	pre·sented	*P-*
pre·fer	*Pfr*	pre·sent·ing	*p*
pref·er·able	*prfrB*	pres·ently	*Pl*
pref·er·ably	*prfrB*	pre·sents (*v.*)	*Ps*
pref·er·ence	*prfrN*	pres·ents (*n.*)	*Ps*
pre·ferred	*Pfr-*	presi·dent	*p*
pre·limi·nary	*Plmre*	presi·den·tial	*Psl*
prem·ises	*prss*	presi·dents	*Ps*
pre·mium	*Pe*	press	*prs*
pre·mi·ums	*Pes*	pressed	*prs-*
pre·paid	*Ppd*	presses	*prss*

press·ing	*prs*	prin·ci·ples	*prNpls*
pres·sure	*prsr*	print	*prN*
pres·sures	*prsrs*	printed	*prN-*
pre·sum·ably	*Pz B*	printer	*prNr*
pre·sume	*Pz*	print·ing	*prN*
pre·sump·tion	*Pzy*	prints	*prÑs*
pretty	*prte*	prior	*prir*
pre·vent	*PvN*	pri·or·ities	*prir ˡs*
pre·ven·tion	*Pvny*	pri·or·ity	*prir ˡ*
pre·view	*Pvru*	pri·vate	*prvt*
pre·vi·ous	*Pves*	privi·lege	*prvlg*
pre·vi·ously	*Pvesl*	privi·leged	*prvlg-*
price	*prs*	privi·leges	*prvlgs*
priced	*prs-*	prize	*prz*
prices	*prss*	prizes	*przs*
pric·ing	*prs*	prob·abil·ity	*PbB ˡ*
pride	*prd*	prob·able	*PbB*
pri·ma·rily	*pr rl*	prob·ably	*PbB*
pri·mary	*pr re*	pro·bate	*Pba*
prime	*pr*	prob·lem	*Pbl*
prin·ci·pal	*prNpl*	prob·lems	*Pbls*
prin·ci·pals	*prNpls*	pro·ce·dure	*Psjr*
prin·ci·ple	*prNpl*	pro·ce·dures	*Psjrs*

pro·ceed	*Psd*	pro·fes·sion·als	*Pfjls*
pro·ceed·ing	*Psd*	pro·fes·sor	*Pfsr*
pro·ceed·ings	*Psd*	pro·fi·ciency	*Pfsne*
pro·ceeds	*Psds*	profit	*Pfl*
pro·cess (v.)	*Pss*	prof·it·able	*PflB*
proc·ess (n.)	*Pss*	prof·its	*Pfls*
proc·essed	*Pss-*	pro·gram	*Pq*
pro·cesses (v.)	*Psss*	pro·grammed	*Pq-*
proc·esses (n.)	*Psss*	pro·gram·ming	*Pq_*
proc·ess·ing	*Pss_*	pro·grams	*Pgs*
pro·cure·ment	*Pcrm*	pro·gress (v.)	*Pgrs*
pro·duce	*Pds*	prog·ress (n.)	*Pgrs*
pro·duced	*Pds-*	pro·gres·sive	*Pgrsv*
pro·ducer	*Pdsr*	pro·hibit	*Phbl*
pro·duc·ers	*Pdsrs*	pro·ject (v.)	*Pjc*
pro·duc·ing	*Pds_*	proj·ect (n.)	*Pjc*
prod·uct	*Pdc*	pro·jected	*Pjc-*
pro·duc·tion	*Pdcy*	pro·jec·tion	*Pjcy*
pro·duc·tive	*Pdcv*	pro·jec·tions	*Pjcys*
pro·duc·tiv·ity	*Pdcv¹*	pro·jec·tor	*Pjcr*
prod·ucts	*Pdcs*	pro·jec·tors	*Pjcrs*
pro·fes·sion	*Pfj*	pro·jects (v.)	*Pjcs*
pro·fes·sional	*Pfjl*	proj·ects (n.)	*Pjcs*

prom·ise	*P—s*	pro·posed	*Ppz-*
prom·ised	*P—s-*	propo·si·tion	*Ppzf*
prom·ises	*P—ss*	pro·rated	*Pra-*
prom·is·ing	*P—s_*	pros·pect	*Pspc*
pro·mote	*P—o*	pro·spec·tive	*Pspcv*
pro·moted	*P—o-*	pros·pects	*Pspcs*
pro·mot·ing	*P—o_*	pro·tect	*Plc*
pro·mo·tion	*P—y*	pro·tected	*Plc-*
pro·mo·tional	*P—yl*	pro·tect·ing	*Plc_*
pro·mo·tions	*P—ys*	pro·tec·tion	*Plcy*
prompt	*P—t*	pro·tec·tive	*Plcv*
promptly	*P—tl*	pro·to·type	*Pllp*
prompt·ness	*P—t'*	proud	*prod*
proof	*prf*	prove	*pv*
proofs	*prfs*	proved	*pv-*
proper	*Ppr*	proven	*pvn*
prop·erly	*Pprl*	proves	*pvs*
prop·er·ties	*prps*	pro·vide	*Pvd*
prop·erty	*prp*	pro·vided	*Pvd-*
pro·por·tion	*Ppry*	provi·dence	*PvdN*
pro·posal	*Ppzl*	pro·vides	*Pvds*
pro·pos·als	*Ppzls*	pro·vid·ing	*Pvd_*
pro·pose	*Ppz*	prov·ince	*Pvn*

pro·vin·cial	*Pvnsl*	pur·chas·ing	*PCs*
prov·ing	*pv*	pure	*pr*
pro·vi·sion	*Pvj*	pur·pose	*Pps*
pro·vi·sions	*Pvjs*	pur·poses	*Ppss*
psy·chi·at·ric	*scelrc*	pur·su·ant	*PsuN*
psy·chology	*sclje*	pur·sue	*Psu*
pub·lic	*pb*	pur·su·ing	*Psu*
pub·li·ca·tion	*pbj*	put	*pt*
pub·li·ca·tions	*pbjs*	put·ting	*pt*
pub·lic·ity	*pbls*		
pub·lish	*pbls*		
pub·lished	*pbls-*	**Q**	
pub·lish·ers	*pblsrs*		
pub·lish·ing	*pbls*	quad·ru·pli·cate	*gdrplcl*
pump	*p~p*	quail	*ql*
pumps	*p~ps*	quali·fi·ca·tion	*qlfj*
punch	*pnC*	quali·fi·ca·tions	*qlfjs*
pu·pils	*ppls*	quali·fied	*qlf-*
pur·chase	*PCs*	qualify	*qlf*
pur·chased	*PCs-*	qual·ity	*ql*
pur·chaser	*PCsr*	quan·ti·ties	*qN*
pur·chas·ers	*PCsrs*	quan·tity	*qN*
pur·chases	*PCss*	quart	*ql*
		quar·ter	*qlr*

quar·ter·back	*qtrbc*	quoted	*qo-*
quar·tered	*qtr-*	quot·ing	*qo̱*
quar·ter·ing	*qtṟ*		
quar·ter·lies	*qtrls*	**R**	
quar·terly	*qtrl*		
quar·ters	*qtrs*	race	*rs*
quarts	*qts*	rack	*rc*
ques·tion	*q*	racks	*rcs*
ques·tion·able	*qʘ*	ra·dia·tion	*rdej*
ques·tioned	*q-*	radio	*rdo*
ques·tion·ing	*q̱-*	ra·dius	*rdes*
ques·tion·naire	*qr*	rail	*rl*
ques·tion·naires	*qrs*	rail·road	*rlrd*
ques·tions	*qs*	rail·roads	*rlrds*
quick	*qc*	rail·way	*rla*
quickly	*qcl*	rain	*rn*
quiet	*qil*	raise	*rz*
quite	*qi*	raised	*rz-*
quota	*qta*	rais·ing	*rẕ-*
quo·tas	*qtas*	ran	*rn*
quo·ta·tion	*qly*	ranch	*rnC*
quo·ta·tions	*qlys*	ran·dom	*rM*
quote	*qo*	range	*rnj*

ranged	*rnj-*	read	*rd*
ranges	*rnjs*	read·able	*rdB*
rang·ing	*rnj_*	reader	*rdr*
rank	*rq*	read·ers	*rdrs*
rapid	*rpd*	readily	*rdl*
rap·idly	*rpdl*	read·ing	*rd_*
rap·ids	*rpds*	read·ings	*rd_*
rare	*rr*	re·ad·mit	*rād-l*
rarely	*rrl*	reads	*rds*
rate	*ra*	ready	*rde*
rated	*ra-*	real	*rl*
rates	*ras*	re·al·is·tic	*relSc*
rather	*rlr*	re·al·ize	*relz*
rat·ing	*ra_*	re·al·ized	*relz-*
ratio	*rso*	really	*rll*
raw	*ra*	re·alty	*relle*
reach	*rC*	rear	*rr*
reached	*rC-*	rea·son	*rzn*
reaches	*rCs*	rea·son·able	*rznB*
reach·ing	*rC_*	rea·son·ably	*rznB*
re·ac·tion	*racy*	rea·son·ing	*rzn_*
re·ac·tions	*racys*	rea·sons	*rzns*
re·ac·tor	*racr*	re·bate	*rba*

re·call	*rcl*	re·cord (*v.*)	*rec*
re·ceipt	*rse*	rec·ord (*n.*)	*rec*
re·ceipts	*rses*	re·corded	*rec-*
re·ceive	*rsv*	re·corder	*recr*
re·ceived	*rsv-*	re·cord·ing	*rec_*
re·ceives	*rsvo*	re·cords (*v.*)	*recs*
re·ceiv·ing	*rsv_*	rec·ords (*n.*)	*recs*
re·cent	*rsN*	re·cover	*rcvr*
re·cently	*rsNl*	re·cov·ered	*rcvr-*
re·cep·tion	*rspy*	re·cov·ery	*rcvre*
reci·pes	*rspes*	rec·rea·tion	*rcrey*
re·cipi·ent	*rspeN*	rec·rea·tional	*rcreyl*
re·cipi·ents	*rspeNs*	re·cruit·ing	*rcru_*
rec·og·ni·tion	*rcgny*	red	*rd*
rec·og·nize	*rcgnz*	re·deemed	*rd-*
rec·og·nized	*rcgnz-*	re·duce	*rds*
rec·og·niz·ing	*rcgnz_*	re·duced	*rds-*
rec·om·mend	*rcm*	re·duces	*rdss*
rec·om·men·da·tion	*rcmy*	re·duc·ing	*rds_*
rec·om·men·da·tions	*rcmys*	re·duc·tion	*rdcy*
rec·om·mended	*rcm-*	re·duc·tions	*rdcys*
rec·om·mend·ing	*rcm_*	refer	*rf*
rec·om·mends	*rcms*	ref·er·ence	*rfN*

ref·er·enced	*rfN-*	re·gional	*rgnl*
ref·er·ences	*rfNs*	re·gions	*rgns*
re·fer·ral	*rfl*	reg·is·ter	*rgSr*
re·fer·rals	*rfls*	reg·is·tered	*rgSr-*
re·ferred	*rf-*	reg·is·ters	*rgSrs*
re·fer·ring	*rf_*	reg·is·tra·tion	*rgSry*
re·fers	*rfs*	re·gret	*rgrl*
re·fin·ing	*rfn_*	re·gret·fully	*rgrlfl*
re·flect	*rflc*	regu·lar	*rglr*
re·flected	*rflc-*	regu·larly	*rglrl*
re·flects	*rflcs*	regu·late	*rgla*
re·form	*rf*	regu·la·tion	*rgly*
re·fund	*rfN*	regu·la·tions	*rglys*
re·funded	*rfN-*	re·ha·bili·ta·tion	*rhbll*
re·funds	*rfNs*	re·im·burse	*r brs*
re·fuse	*rfz*	re·im·bursed	*r brs-*
re·fused	*rfz-*	re·im·burse·ment	*r brsm*
re·gard	*re*	re·in·forced	*rnfs-*
re·garded	*re-*	re·in·state	*rnSa*
re·gard·ing	*re_*	re·in·stated	*rnSa-*
re·gard·less	*rels*	re·in·state·ment	*rnSam*
re·gards	*res*	re·in·sur·ance	*rins*
re·gion	*rgn*	re·it·er·ate	*rilra*

re·ject	*rjc*	re·lo·ca·tion	*rlcy*
re·jected	*rjc-*	re·luc·tant	*rlctM*
re·jec·tion	*rjcy*	rely	*rli*
re·late	*rla*	re·main	*r_m*
re·lated	*rla-*	re·main·der	*r_Mr*
re·lates	*rlas*	re·mained	*r_n-*
re·lat·ing	*rla_*	re·main·ing	*r_n_*
re·la·tion	*rly*	re·mains	*r_ms*
re·la·tions	*rlys*	re·mark·able	*r_rcB*
re·la·tion·ship	*rlys*	re·marks	*r_rcs*
re·la·tion·ships	*rlyss*	remedy	*r_de*
rela·tive	*rlv*	re·mem·ber	*rmbr*
rela·tively	*rlvl*	re·mind	*rm*
relay	*rla*	re·minded	*rm-*
re·lease	*rls*	re·minder	*rmr*
re·leased	*rls-*	re·mind·ers	*rmrs*
re·leases	*rlss*	re·mit·tance	*r_lM*
rele·vant	*rlvM*	re·mit·ted	*r_l-*
re·li·able	*rliB*	re·mit·ting	*r_l_*
re·lief	*rlf*	re·moval	*r_vl*
re·lieved	*rlv-*	re·move	*r_v*
re·lig·ion	*rlyn*	re·moved	*r_v-*
re·lig·ious	*rlys*	re·mov·ing	*r_v_*

ren·dered	*rNr-*	re·placed	*rpls-*
ren·der·ing	*rNr*	re·place·ment	*rplsm*
renew	*rnu*	re·place·ments	*rplsms*
re·newal	*rnul*	re·plac·ing	*rpls*
re·newed	*rnu-*	re·plies	*rplis*
rent	*rN*	reply	*rpli*
rental	*rNl*	re·ply·ing	*rpli*
rent·als	*rNls*	re·port	*rpl*
rent·ing	*rN*	re·ported	*rpl-*
re·or·der	*rod*	re·port·edly	*rpl-l*
re·or·dered	*rod-*	re·porter	*rplr*
re·or·gan·iza·tion	*rogj*	re·port·ers	*rplrs*
re·or·gan·ize	*rog*	re·port·ing	*rpl*
re·or·gan·ized	*rog-*	re·ports	*rpls*
re·or·gan·izes	*rogs*	rep·re·sent	*rep*
re·or·gan·iz·ing	*rog-*	rep·re·sen·ta·tion	*repj*
re·pair	*rpr*	rep·re·sen·ta·tive	*rep*
re·paired	*rpr-*	rep·re·sen·ta·tives	*reps*
re·pair·ing	*rpr*	rep·re·sented	*rep-*
re·pairs	*rprs*	rep·re·sent·ing	*rep*
re·pay·ment	*rpam*	rep·re·sents	*reps*
re·peat	*rpe*	re·print	*rprN*
re·place	*rpls*	re·prints	*rprNs*

re·pro·duce	*rᵖds*	res·er·va·tions	*rzrvjs*
re·pro·duc·tion	*rᵖdcj*	re·serve	*rzrv*
re·prove	*rpv*	re·served	*rzrv-*
re·proved	*rpv-*	re·serves	*rzrvs*
re·proves	*rpvs*	resi·dence	*rzdN*
re·prov·ing	*rpv̱*	resi·dency	*rzdNe*
repu·ta·tion	*rptj*	resi·dent	*rzdN*
re·quest	*rqs*	resi·den·tial	*rzdnsl*
re·quested	*rqs-*	resi·dents	*rzdNs*
re·quest·ing	*rqs̱*	res·ig·na·tion	*rzgnj*
re·quests	*rqss*	re·sis·tance	*rzSN*
re·quire	*rq*	reso·lu·tion	*rzlj*
re·quired	*rq-*	reso·lu·tions	*rzljs*
re·quire·ment	*rqm*	re·solve	*rzlv*
re·quire·ments	*rqms*	re·solved	*rzlv-*
re·quires	*rqs*	re·source	*rsrs*
re·quir·ing	*rq_*	re·sources	*rsrss*
req·ui·si·tion	*rqzj*	re·spect	*rspc*
req·ui·si·tions	*rqzjs*	re·spected	*rspc-*
re·sale	*rsl*	re·spect·fully	*rspcfl*
re·sched·ule	*rscjl*	re·spec·tive	*rspcv*
re·search	*rSC*	re·spec·tively	*rspcvl*
res·er·va·tion	*rzrvj*	re·spects	*rspcs*

re·spond	*rsp*	re·tail·ers	*rtlrs*
re·sponded	*rsp-*	re·tain	*rtn*
re·spond·ing	*rsp̲*	re·tained	*rtn-*
re·sponds	*rsps*	re·tain·ing	*rtn̲*
re·sponse	*rsp*	re·tard·ing	*rtrd̲*
re·spon·si·bil·ities	*rspθ ⁶*	re·ten·tion	*rtnj*
re·spon·si·bil·ity	*rspθ ˡ*	re·tire	*rtr*
re·spon·si·ble	*rspθ*	re·tired	*rtr-*
re·spon·sive	*rspv*	re·tire·ment	*rtrm*
rest	*rδ*	re·turn	*rel*
res·tau·rant	*rSrN*	re·turned	*rel-*
res·to·ra·tion	*rSrj*	re·turn·ing	*rel̲*
re·store	*rSr*	re·turns	*rels*
re·strict	*rSrc*	re·veal	*rvl*
re·stricted	*rSrc-*	re·vealed	*rvl-*
re·stric·tions	*rSrcjs*	reve·nue	*rvnu*
re·sult	*rzll*	reve·nues	*rvnus*
re·sulted	*rzll-*	re·verse	*rvrs*
re·sult·ing	*rzll̲*	re·view	*rvu*
re·sults	*rzlls*	re·viewed	*rvu-*
re·sume	*rz⌣*	re·view·ing	*rvu̲*
resumé	*rz⌣a*	re·views	*rvus*
re·tail	*rtl*	re·vised	*rvz-*

Word	Shorthand	Word	Shorthand
re·vi·sion	_rvy_	rock	_rc_
re·vi·sions	_rvys_	rocket	_rct_
revo·lu·tion	_rvly_	rocky	_rce_
revo·lu·tion·ary	_rvlyre_	rodeo	_rdo_
re·ward	_rw_	role	_rl_
re·ward·ing	_rw_	roll	_rl_
re·writ·ten	_rrtn_	rolled	_rl-_
rib·bon	_rbn_	rolls	_rls_
rib·bons	_rbns_	roof	_rf_
rich	_rC_	room	_r_
rider	_rdr_	rooms	_r-s_
right	_ru_	rose	_rz_
rights	_rus_	ro·tary	_rtre_
rigid	_ryd_	rough	_rf_
ring	_rg_	round	_roN_
rings	_rgs_	route	_ru_ (N.V.) _rot_ (N.V.)
rise	_rz_	routes	_rus_
ris·ing	_rz-_	rou·tine	_rtn_
risk	_rsc_	rout·ing	_ru_ (N.V.) _rot_ (N.V)
risks	_rscs_	row	_ro_
river	_rvr_	roy·alty	_rylle_
road	_rd_	rub·ber	_rbr_
roads	_rds_	rug	_rg_

rule	*rl*	sale·able	*slb*
rules	*rls*	sales	*sls*
rul·ing	*rl*	sales·man	*slsm*
run	*rn*	sales·man·ship	*slsms*
run·ning	*rn*	sales·men	*slsm*
runs	*rns*	sales·per·son	*slspsn*
rup·ture	*rpCr*	sales·woman	*slsm*
rush	*rs*	sales·women	*slsm*
rust	*rs*	salt	*sll*
		same	*s*

S

		sam·ple	*sa*
		sam·ples	*sas*
safe	*sf*	sand	*sN*
safely	*sfl*	sand·wich	*sNC*
safety	*sfle*	sani·tary	*sntre*
said	*sd*	sat·is·fac·tion	*saly*
sail·ing	*sl*	sat·is·fac·to·rily	*sall*
saint	*sN*	sat·is·fac·tory	*sal*
sake	*sc*	sat·is·fied	*sal-*
sala·ried	*slre-*	sat·is·fies	*sals*
sala·ries	*slres*	sat·isfy	*sal*
salary	*slre*	sat·is·fy·ing	*sal*
sale	*sl*	save	*sv*

saved	*sv-*	sci·en·tific	*sinlfc*
saves	*svs*	scope	*scp*
sav·ing	*sv̰*	score	*scr*
sav·ings	*sv̰*	scores	*scrs*
saw	*sa*	scotch	*scl*
say	*sa*	screen	*scrn*
say·ing	*sa̰*	screens	*scrns*
say·ings	*sa̰*	script	*S*
says	*sz*	scripts	*Ss*
scale	*scl*	sea	*se*
scan·ning	*scn̰*	seal	*sl*
scat·tered	*sclr-*	seals	*sls*
scene	*sn*	sea·port	*sepl*
sched·ule	*scjl*	sea·ports	*sepls*
sched·uled	*scjl-*	search	*SC*
sched·ules	*scjls*	sea·side	*sesd*
sched·ul·ing	*scjl̰*	sea·son	*szn*
schol·ar·ship	*sclrs*	sea·sonal	*sznl*
schol·ar·ships	*sclrss*	sea·sons	*szns*
school	*scl*	seat	*se*
schools	*scls*	seats	*ses*
sci·ence	*siN*	sec·ond	*sec 2d*
sci·ences	*siNs*	sec·on·dary	*secre*

sec·onded	*sec -*	seemed	*s -*
sec·ond·hand	*sechN*	seems	*s s*
sec·ond·ing	*sec*	seen	*sn*
sec·ondly	*secl*	sel·dom	*sld*
sec·onds	*secs*	se·lect	*slc*
sec·re·tarial	*secl*	se·lected	*slc -*
sec·re·tar·ies	*secs*	se·lect·ing	*slc*
sec·re·tary	*sec*	se·lec·tion	*slcy*
sec·tion	*scy*	se·lec·tions	*slcys*
sec·tions	*scys*	se·lec·tive	*slcv*
sec·tor	*scr*	self	*sf*
se·cure	*scr*	self-addressed	*sfadrs -*
se·cured	*scr -*	self-assurance	*sfasrN*
se·cur·ing	*scr*	self-confidence	*sfkfdN*
se·cu·ri·ties	*scr ʳ*	self-defense	*sfdfN*
se·cu·rity	*scr ʳ*	self-explanatory	*sfxplnlre*
see	*se*	self-improvement	*sf pvm*
seed	*sd*	self-made	*sf d*
see·ing	*se*	sell	*sl*
seek	*sc*	sell·ers	*slrs*
seek·ing	*sc*	sell·ing	*sl*
seeks	*scs*	sells	*sls*
seem	*s*	se·mes·ter	*s Sr*

semi·nar	*smr*	ser·mon	*Sm*
semi·nars	*smrs*	serve	*Sv*
sen·ate	*snt*	served	*Sv-*
sena·tor	*sntr*	serves	*Svs*
sena·tors	*sntrs*	serv·ice	*Svs*
send	*sN*	serv·ice·man	*Svsm*
send·ing	*sN̲*	serv·ice·men	*Svsm*
sen·ior	*sr*	serv·ices	*Svss*
sen·ior·ity	*sr^l*	serv·ice·woman	*Svs m*
sen·iors	*srs*	serv·ice·women	*Svsm*
sense	*sN*	serv·ing	*Sv̲*
senses	*sNs*	ses·sion	*sj*
sen·si·tive	*sNv*	ses·sions	*sjs*
sent	*sN*	set	*st*
sen·tence	*sNN*	sets	*sts*
sepa·rate	*v.* *spra* *adj.* *sprt*	set·ting	*st̲*
sepa·rately	*sprtl*	set·tle	*stl*
sepa·ra·tion	*spry*	set·tled	*stl-*
se·quen·tial	*sqnsl*	set·tle·ment	*stlm*
se·rial	*srel*	set·tle·ments	*stlms*
se·ries	*srz*	sev·eral	*sv*
se·ri·ous	*sres*	se·vere	*svr*
se·ri·ously	*sresl*	se·verely	*svrl*

sewer	_sur_	shifts	_sfts_
shade	_sd_	ship	_s_
shaft	_sft_	ship·ment	_sm_
shall	_sl_	ship·ments	_sms_
shape	_sp_	shipped	_s-_
shapes	_sps_	ship·per	_sr_
share	_sr_	ship·pers	_srs_
shared	_sr-_	ship·ping	_s_
share·holder	_srhldr_	ships	_ss_
share·hold·ers	_srhldrs_	ship·yards	_syds_
shares	_srs_	shirts	_srts_
shar·ing	_sr_	shocked	_sc-_
sharp	_srp_	shoe	_su_
sharply	_srpl_	shoes	_sus_
she	_se_	shoot	_su_
sheep	_sp_	shoot·ing	_su_
sheet	_se_	shop	_sp_
sheets	_ses_	shop·ping	_sp_
shelf	_slf_	shops	_sps_
shell	_sl_	short	_srt_
shelves	_slvs_	short·age	_srj_
shift	_sft_	short·ages	_srjs_
shift·ing	_sft_	shorter	_srr_

short·hand	*srhN*	sig·na·ture	*sig*
shortly	*srll*	sig·na·tures	*sigs*
shorts	*srls*	signed	*sn-*
shot	*sl*	sig·nifi·cance	*sig*
should	*sd*	sig·nifi·cant	*sig*
shouldn't	*sdN*	sig·nifi·cantly	*sigl*
show	*so*	sign·ing	*sn*
showed	*so-*	signs	*sns*
shower	*sor*	sili·con	*slk*
show·ing	*so_*	sil·ver	*slvr*
show·ings	*so=*	simi·lar	*s lr*
shown	*sn*	simi·larly	*s lrl*
shows	*soo*	sim·ple	*s pl*
shut	*sl*	sim·plic·ity	*s pls'*
shut·down	*sldon*	sim·pli·fied	*s plf-*
sick	*sc*	sim·ply	*s pl*
sick·ness	*sc'*	since	*sN*
side	*sd*	sin·cere	*snsr*
sides	*sds*	sin·cerely	*snsrl*
sight	*si*	sin·gle	*sgl*
sign	*sn*	sis·ter	*sSr*
sig·nal	*sgnl*	sis·ters	*sSrs*
sig·nals	*sgnls*	sit	*sl*

Word	Shorthand	Word	Shorthand
site	*si*	slightly	*slil*
sites	*sis*	slip	*slp*
situ·ate	*sil*	slips	*slps*
situ·ated	*sil-*	slow	*slo*
situ·ates	*sils*	small	*sml*
situ·at·ing	*sil*	smaller	*smlr*
situ·ation	*sily*	smocks	*smcs*
situ·ations	*silys*	smoke	*smc*
siz·able	*szb*	smooth	*smt*
size	*sz*	smoothly	*smtl*
sized	*sz-*	snow	*sno*
sizes	*szs*	so	*so*
sketch	*scC*	soap	*sp*
ski	*sce*	so·cial	*ssl*
ski·ing	*sce*	so·ci·ety	*ssi'*
skill	*scl*	sock	*sc*
skilled	*scl-*	sod	*sd*
skills	*scls*	soft	*sft*
slab	*slb*	soil	*syl*
slacks	*slcs*	soils	*syls*
sleeves	*slvs*	sold	*sld*
slides	*slds*	sole	*sl*
slight	*sli*	solely	*sll*

soles	*sls*	source	*srs*
solid	*sld*	sources	*srss*
so·lu·tion	*slf*	south	*S*
so·lu·tions	*slfs*	south·east	*SE*
solve	*slv*	south·east·erly	*SErl*
solved	*slv-*	south·east·ern	*SErn*
sol·vent	*slvn*	south·erly	*Srl*
solv·ing	*slv̠*	south·ern	*Srn*
some	*s*	south·ward	*Sw*
some·body	*s bde*	south·west	*SW*
some·one	*s ı*	south·west·ern	*SWrn*
some·thing	*s̠*	space	*sps*
some·time	*s t*	spaces	*spss*
some·times	*s ts*	spac·ing	*sps̠*
some·what	*s t*	spank	*spq*
some·where	*s r*	spare	*spr*
son	*sn*	sparks	*sprcs*
sons	*sns*	speak	*spc*
soon	*sn*	speaker	*spcr*
sooner	*snr*	speak·ers	*spcrs*
sorry	*sre*	speak·ing	*spc̠*
sort	*srl*	speaks	*spcs*
sound	*son*	spe·cial	*spsl*

spe·cial·ist	*spsls*	splen·did	*splNd*
spe·cial·ists	*spslss*	split	*spll*
spe·cial·ized	*spslz-*	spoke	*spc*
spe·cially	*spsll*	spon·sor	*spNr*
spe·cials	*spsls*	spon·sored	*spNr-*
spe·cialty	*spslle*	spon·sor·ing	*spNr̲*
spe·cific	*sp*	spon·sors	*spNrs*
spe·cif·ically	*spl*	spon·sor·ship	*spNrs*
speci·fi·ca·tion	*spj*	spools	*spls*
speci·fi·ca·tions	*spjs*	sport	*spl*
speci·fied	*sp-*	sports	*spls*
speci·fies	*sps*	spot	*spl*
specify	*sp*	spots	*spls*
speci·fy·ing	*sp̲*	spouse	*spos*
speci·men	*spsm*	spray	*spra*
speech	*spC*	spread	*sprd*
speed	*spd*	spree	*spre*
speeds	*spds*	spring	*sprq*
spend	*spN*	springs	*sprqs*
spend·ing	*spN̲*	sprin·kler	*sprqlr*
spent	*spN̄*	sprocket	*sprcl*
spirit	*sprl*	sprock·ets	*sprcls*
spite	*spi*	square	*sq*

squared	*sq-*	stan·dard·ized	*Sdz-*
squares	*sqs*	stan·dard·izes	*Sdzs*
squar·est	*sqs*	stan·dard·iz·ing	*Sdz-*
squar·ing	*sq-*	stan·dards	*Sds*
sta·bil·ity	*SB'*	stand·ing	*Sn*
sta·ble	*SB*	stand·point	*Snpy*
stack	*Sc*	stands	*Sns*
staff	*Sf*	sta·ples	*Spls*
staffed	*Sf-*	star·board	*Srbrd*
staff·ing	*Sf-*	stars	*Srs*
staffs	*Sfs*	start	*Srt*
stage	*Sj*	started	*Srt-*
stages	*Sjs*	starter	*Srtr*
stain·less	*Snls*	start·ing	*Srt-*
stake	*Sc*	starts	*Srts*
stamp	*S—p*	state	*Sa*
stamped	*S—p-*	stated	*Sa-*
stamp·ing	*S—p-*	state·ment	*Sam*
stamps	*S—ps*	state·ments	*Sams*
stand	*Sn*	states	*Sas*
stan·dard	*Sd*	static	*Stc*
stan·dard·iza·tion	*Sdy*	stat·ing	*Sa-*
stan·dard·ize	*Sdz*	sta·tion	*Sj*

sta·tioner	_Sjr_	steps	_Sps_
sta·tion·ery	_Sjre_	ster·ling	_Srlg_
sta·tions	_Sjs_	stew·ard·ess	_Sws_
sta·tis·tic	_StSc_	stew·ard·ship	_Sws_
sta·tis·ti·cal	_StScl_	sticker	_Scr_
sta·tis·tics	_StScs_	still	_Sl_
status	_Sts_	stimu·late	_S la_
statue	_SCu_	stimu·lat·ing	_S la_
stat·utes	_SCus_	sti·pend	_SpN_
stay	_Sa_	stipu·lated	_Spla-_
stay·ing	_Sa_	stock	_Sc_
steadily	_Sdl_	stock·hold·ers	_Schldrs_
steady	_Sde_	stock·ing	_Sc_
steam	_S_	stock·pile	_Scpl_
steam·ship	_S_	stocks	_Scs_
steel	_Sl_	stock·yards	_Scyds_
steer·ing	_Sr_	stop	_Sp_
stem	_S_	stop·ping	_Sp_
sten·cil	_SNl_	stor·age	_Srj_
sten·cil·ing	_SNl_	store	_Sr_
sten·cils	_SNls_	stored	_Sr-_
ste·nog·ra·phers	_Sngrfrs_	stores	_Srs_
step	_Sp_	sto·ries	_Sres_

story	_Sre_	stu·dents	_SdNs_
straight	_Sra_	stud·ied	_Sde-_
straighten	_Sran_	stud·ies	_Sdes_
stream	_Sr_	study	_Sde_
street	_S_	study·ing	_Sde_
street·car	_Scr_	style	_Sl_
streets	_Ss_	styled	_Sl-_
strength	_Srql_	styles	_Sls_
strengthen	_Srqln_	sub·com·mit·tee	_sk_
stress	_Srs_	sub·com·mit·tees	_sks_
strict	_Src_	sub·con·scious	_skss_
strictly	_Srcl_	sub·di·vi·sion	_sdvy_
strike	_Src_	sub·ject	_syc_
strip	_Srp_	sub·jects	_sycs_
strips	_Srps_	sub·ma·rine	_s rn_
strive	_Srv_	sub·mis·sion	_s y_
strong	_Srq_	sub·mit	_s l_
strongly	_Srql_	sub·mit·ted	_s l-_
struc·tural	_SrcCrl_	sub·mit·ting	_s l_
struc·ture	_SrcCr_	sub·scribe	_sS_
struc·tures	_SrcCrs_	sub·scriber	_sSr_
stub	_Sb_	sub·scrib·ers	_sSrs_
stu·dent	_SdN_	sub·scribes	_sSs_

sub·scrib·ing	_sS_	suf·fi·cient	_sfsN_
sub·scrip·tion	_sSy_	suf·fi·ciently	_sfsNl_
sub·scrip·tions	_sSys_	sugar	_sgr_
sub·se·quent	_ssqN_	sug·gest	_sug_
sub·se·quently	_ssqNl_	sug·gested	_sug-_
sub·sidi·ar·ies	_ssderes_	sug·gest·ing	_sug_
sub·sidi·ary	_ssdere_	sug·ges·tion	_sugy_
sub·sis·tence	_ssSN_	sug·ges·tions	_sugys_
sub·stan·dard	_sSd_	sug·gests	_sugs_
sub·stan·tial	_sSnsl_	suit	_su_
sub·stan·tially	_sSnsll_	suit·abil·ity	_suB^l_
sub·stan·ti·ate	_sSnsa_	suit·able	_suB_
sub·sti·tute	_sSlu_	suited	_su-_
sub·urbs	_srbs_	suits	_sus_
suc·ceed	_scsd_	sum	_s_
suc·cess	_suc_	sum·ma·ries	_s~res_
suc·cesses	_sucs_	sum·mary	_s~re_
suc·cess·ful	_sucf_	sum·mer	_s~r_
suc·cess·fully	_sucfl_	sum·mons	_sms_
such	_sC_	super	_S_
sud·den	_sdn_	su·per·in·ten·dent	_S_
sud·denly	_sdnl_	su·per·in·ten·dents	_Ss_
suf·fered	_sfr-_	su·pe·rior	_sprer_

su·per·mar·ket	_S~r_	sup·pose	_sp3_
su·per·vise	_Sv3_	sup·posed	_sp3-_
su·per·vised	_Sv3-_	su·preme	_spr_
su·per·vis·ing	_Sv3_	sur·charge	_SG_
su·per·vi·sion	_Sv7_	sure	_sr_
su·per·vi·sor	_Svzr_	surely	_srl_
su·per·vi·sors	_Svzrs_	sur·face	_Sfs_
su·per·vi·sory	_Svzre_	sur·faces	_Sfss_
sup·ple·ment	_splm_	sur·geon	_Sjn_
sup·ple·men·tal	_splml_	sur·gery	_Sjre_
sup·ple·men·tary	_splmre_	sur·gi·cal	_Sjcl_
sup·ple·ments	_splms_	sur·plus	_Spls_
sup·plied	_spli-_	sur·pluses	_Splss_
sup·plier	_splir_	sur·prise	_Sprz_
sup·pli·ers	_splirs_	sur·prised	_Sprz-_
sup·plies	_splis_	sur·ren·der	_SNr_
sup·ply	_spli_	sur·round	_SoN_
sup·ply·ing	_spli_	sur·round·ing	_SoN_
sup·port	_spl_	sur·vey	_Sva_
sup·ported	_spl-_	sur·veyor	_Svar_
sup·porter	_splr_	sur·veys	_Svas_
sup·port·ing	_spl_	sur·viv·ing	_Svv_
sup·ports	_spls_	sus·pect	_sspc_

Word	Shorthand	Word	Shorthand
sus·pense	*sspN*	take	*lc*
sus·pen·sion	*sspny*	taken	*lcn*
sus·tained	*sSn-*	takes	*lcs*
sweep·stakes	*s plcs*	tak·ing	*lc*
switch	*s C*	tal·ent	*len*
switches	*s Cs*	tal·ents	*lens*
switch·ing	*s C*	talk	*lc*
sym·bol	*s B*	talked	*lc-*
sym·pa·thetic	*s pllc*	talk·ing	*lc*
sym·pa·thize	*s plz*	talks	*lcs*
sym·pa·thy	*s ple*	tank	*lq*
syn·thetic	*snllc*	tanks	*lqs*
sys·tem	*sl*	tap	*lp*
sys·tem·atic	*sl lc*	tape	*lp*
sys·tems	*sls*	tapes	*lps*
		tap·ping	*lp-*

T

Word	Shorthand	Word	Shorthand
		tar	*lr*
		tar·iff	*lrf*
table	*lB*	task	*lsc*
ta·bles	*lBs*	tax	*lx*
tag	*lq*	tax·able	*lxB*
tags	*lqs*	taxa·tion	*lxy*
tai·lored	*lr-*	taxed	*lx-*

taxes	*Lxs*	tele·vi·sion	*Uvy*
tax·payer	*Lxpar*	tell	*Ul*
teach	*UC*	tell·ing	*Ul̠*
teacher	*UCr*	tells	*Uls*
teach·ers	*UCrs*	tem·pera·ture	*LprCr*
teach·ing	*UC̠*	tem·pera·tures	*LprCrs*
team	*L*	tempo	*Lpo*
tea·pot	*lepl*	tem·po·rarily	*Lprrl*
tear	*lr*	tem·po·rary	*Lprre*
tech·ni·cal	*lcncl*	ten·ant	*LnN*
tech·ni·cally	*lcncll*	ten·ants	*LnNs*
tech·ni·cian	*lcny*	tend	*LN*
tech·ni·cians	*lcnys*	ten·ta·tive	*LNv*
tech·nique	*lcnc*	ten·ta·tively	*LNvl*
tech·niques	*lcncs*	term	*lr*
tech·nology	*lcnlge*	ter·mi·nal	*lrml*
teen·age	*lnay*	ter·mi·nals	*lrmls*
teeth	*Ul*	ter·mi·nate	*lrma*
tele·gram	*Ulg*	ter·mi·nated	*lrma-*
tele·graph	*Ulgrf*	ter·mi·na·tion	*lrmy*
tele·phone	*Ulfn*	terms	*lr~s*
tele·phones	*Ulfns*	ter·race	*lrs*
tele·type	*Ullp*	ter·ri·ble	*lrß*

Word	Shorthand	Word	Shorthand
ter·ri·to·ries		theirs	
ter·ri·tory		them	
test		theme	
tested		them·selves	
tes·ti·fied		then	
tes·ti·mony		theory	
test·ing		thera·pist	
tests		therapy	
text		there	
text·book		there·af·ter	
text·books		thereby	
tex·tile		there·fore	
texts		therein	
than		thereof	
thank		thereon	
thank·ing		thereto	
thanks		there·to·fore	
that		ther·mal	
that's		ther·mo·stats	
the		these	
thea·ter		they	
theft		they'll	
their		they're	

Word		Word	
they've		tidal	
thick		tie	
thin		tied	
thing		tile	
things		time	
think		timely	
think·ing		times	
this		time·ta·ble	
thor·ough		time·ta·bles	
thor·oughly		tim·ing	
those		tip	
though		tips	
thought		tire	
thought·ful		tires	
thoughts		title	
thou·sand		ti·tled	
thou·sands		ti·tles	
thou·sandth		to	
through		today	
through·out		to·gether	
thus		token	
ticket		told	
tick·ets		to·mor·row	

ton	*ln*	tower	*lor*
ton·nage	*lny*	town	*lon*
tons	*lns*	town·ship	*lons*
too	*l*	toy	*ly*
took	*lc*	track	*lrc*
tool	*ll*	tracks	*lrcs*
tools	*lls*	tract	*lrc*
tooth	*ll*	trac·tor	*lrclr*
top	*lp*	trade	*lrd*
topic	*lpc*	trad·ing	*lrd*
top·ics	*lpcs*	tra·di·tions	*lrdjs*
total	*lol*	traf·fic	*lrfc*
to·taled	*lol-*	trailer	*lrlr*
to·tal·ing	*lol*	trail·ers	*lrlrs*
to·tally	*loll*	train	*lrn*
to·tals	*lols*	trained	*lrn-*
touch	*lc*	trainee	*lrne*
tough	*lf*	train·ing	*lrn*
tour	*lr*	trains	*lrns*
tour·na·ment	*lrnm*	tran·quil	*Tql*
tours	*lrs*	trans·act	*Tac*
to·ward	*lw*	trans·ac·tion	*Tacy*
to·wards	*lws*	trans·ac·tions	*Tacys*

Word	Shorthand	Word	Shorthand
tran·scribe	TS	trav·el·ing	lrvl
tran·script	TS	trav·els	lrvls
trans·fer	Tfr	treas·ure	lrzr
trans·ferred	Tfr-	treas·urer	lrzrs
trans·fer·ring	Tfr_	treas·ury	lrzre
trans·fers	Tfrs	treat	lre
trans·former	Tfr	treated	lre-
trans·form·ers	Tfrs	trea·ties	lrles
tran·sis·tor	TSr	treat·ment	lrem
tran·sis·tors	TSrs	treaty	lrle
tran·sit	Tl	tree	lre
tran·si·tion	Tj	trees	lres
trans·la·tion	Tlj	tre·men·dous	lrmds
trans·mis·sion	Tj	trend	lrN
trans·mit·tal	Tll	trends	lrNs
trans·plant	TplN	trial	lril
trans·port	Tpl	tri·an·gle	lrigl
trans·por·ta·tion	Tplj	tribu·tar·ies	lrbtres
trans·ported	Tpl-	tried	lri-
trans·porter	Tplr	trip	lrp
trans·port·ing	Tpl_	trips	lrps
trans·ports	Tpls	trouble	lrB
travel	lrvl	truck	lrc

trucks	_Lrcs_	type·writ·ing	_Lpru_
true	_Lru_	typ·ical	_Lpcl_
truly	_Lrul_	typ·ing	_Lp_
trust	_LrS_	typ·ists	_LpSs_
trus·tee	_LrSe_		
trus·tees	_LrSes_		
trust·ing	_LrS_	**U**	
trusts	_LrSs_	ul·ti·mate	_ult_
truth	_Lrl_	ul·ti·mately	_ult_ll_
try	_Lru_	un·able	_uB_
try·ing	_Lru_	unani·mously	_unn_sl_
tube	_Ub_	un·au·thor·ized	_ualrz_
tub·ing	_Ub_	un·cer·tain	_uSln_
tui·tion	_luy_	un·changed	_uCny-_
turn	_Lrn_	under	_U_
turned	_Lrn-_	un·der·cur·rent	_UcrN_
turn·ing	_Lrn_	un·der·go·ing	_Ug_
turn·over	_LrnO_	un·der·gradu·ate	_Ugrjul_
twin	_Ln_	un·der·ground	_UgroN_
type	_Lp_	un·der·handed	_UhN-_
typed	_Lp-_	un·der·lie·	_Uli_
types	_Lps_	un·der·line	_Uln_
type·writer	_Lprur_	un·der·lined	_Uln-_

un·der·lines	*Ulns*	un·der·writ·ing	*Uri*
un·der·ly·ing	*Uli*	un·dis·trib·uted	*uD-*
un·der·mine	*Um*	un·di·vided	*udvd-*
un·der·neath	*Unl*	un·doubt·edly	*udotl*
un·der·score	*Uscr*	undue	*udu*
un·der·scored	*Uscr-*	un·earned	*uern-*
un·der·scores	*Uscrs*	un·em·ployed	*up-*
un·der·scor·ing	*Uscr*	un·em·ploy·ment	*upm*
un·der·signed	*Usn-*	un·fair	*ufr*
un·der·stand	*USN*	un·for·tu·nate	*ufCnl*
un·der·stand·able	*USNB*	un·for·tu·nately	*ufCnll*
un·der·stand·ably	*USNB*	un·grate·ful	*ugrf*
un·der·stand·ing	*USN*	uni·form	*unf*
un·der·stood	*Usd*	uni·for·mity	*unf*
un·der·take	*Ulc*	un·im·por·tant	*upl*
un·der·taken	*Ulcn*	union	*unyn*
un·der·takes	*Ulcs*	un·ions	*unyns*
un·der·tak·ing	*Ulc*	unique	*unc*
un·der·took	*Ulc*	unit	*unl*
un·der·way	*Ua*	united	*uni-*
un·der·write	*Uri*	units	*unls*
un·der·writer	*Urir*	uni·ver·sal	*unvrsl*
un·der·writ·ers	*Urirs*	uni·ver·si·ties	*Us*

uni·ver·sity	*U*	un·will·ing·ness	*ul'*
un·less	*uls*	up	*p*
un·like	*ulc*	up·dated	*pda-*
un·load·ing	*uld*	upon	*po*
un·nec·es·sarily	*unesl*	upper	*pr*
un·nec·es·sary	*unes*	up·ward	*pw*
un·or·gan·ized	*uog-*	urban	*urbn*
un·paid	*upd*	urge	*ury*
un·prof·it·able	*uflß*	urged	*ury-*
un·rea·son·able	*urznß*	ur·gency	*uryñe*
un·re·spon·sive	*urspv*	ur·gent	*uryñ*
un·sat·is·fac·to·rily	*usall*	urg·ing	*ury-*
un·sat·is·fac·tory	*usal*	us	*s*
un·sat·is·fied	*usal-*	usage	*usy*
un·suc·cess·ful	*usucf*	use	*už* (v.) *ûs* (n.)
un·suc·cess·fully	*usucfl*	used	*uz-*
until	*ull*	use·ful	*usf*
un·used	*uuz-*	use·less	*usls*
un·usual	*uuz*	user	*uzr*
un·usu·ally	*uuzl*	users	*uzrs*
un·wel·come	*ulk*	uses	*užš* (v.) *ûss* (n.)
un·will·ing	*ul-*	using	*uz-*
un·will·ingly	*ulf*	usual	*uz*

usu·ally	*uzl*
util·ities	*utl⁶*
util·ity	*utl¹*
util·iza·tion	*utlz*
util·ize	*utlz*
util·ized	*utlz-*
util·iz·ing	*utlz-*
ut·most	*ut-ᔆ*

V

va·can·cies	*vcNes*
va·cancy	*vcNe*
va·cant	*vcN*
va·ca·tion	*vcj*
va·ca·tions	*vcjs*
vacuum	*vcy*
valid	*vld*
va·lid·ity	*vld¹*
val·ley	*vle*
valu·able	*vluß*
valu·ation	*vluy*
value	*vlu*

val·ued	*vlu-*
val·ues	*vlus*
valve	*vlv*
valves	*vlvs*
van	*vn*
van·dal·ism	*vNlz*
vapor	*vpr*
vari·able	*vreß*
var·ied	*vre-*
var·ies	*vres*
va·ri·eties	*vri⁶*
va·ri·ety	*vri¹*
vari·ous	*vres*
vary	*vre*
vast	*vᔆ*
ve·hi·cle	*vhcl*
ve·hi·cles	*vhcls*
ven·dor	*vNr*
ven·ture	*vnCr*
ver·bal	*vrß*
veri·fi·ca·tion	*vrff*
veri·fied	*vrf-*
verify	*vrf*

veri·fy·ing	*vrf-*	vir·tu·ally	*vrCull*
ver·sa·til·ity	*vrstl*	visa	*vza*
ver·sion	*vrq*	vis·ible	*vzβ*
ver·sus	*vrss*	vi·sion	*vq*
ver·ti·cal	*vrtcl*	visit	*vzt*
very	*v*	vis·ited	*vzt-*
ves·sel	*vsl*	vis·it·ing	*vzt_*
ves·sels	*vsls*	visi·tor	*vztr*
vested	*vs-*	visi·tors	*vztrs*
vet·er·ans	*vtrns*	vis·its	*vzts*
vexa·tion	*vxy*	visual	*vzul*
via	*va*	vital	*vtl*
vice	*vo*	vo·ca·tional	*vcjl*
vice presi·dent	*VP*	voice	*vys*
vice presi·den·tial	*VPsl*	volt	*vll*
vice presi·dents	*VPs*	volt·age	*vlly*
vi·cin·ity	*vsn*	vol·ume	*vol*
view	*vu*	vol·umes	*vols*
view·ers	*vurs*	vol·un·tary	*vlntre*
views	*vus*	vol·un·teer	*vlntr*
vil·lage	*vlj*	vol·un·teers	*vlntrs*
vio·la·tion	*vrly*	vote	*vo*
vio·la·tions	*vrljs*	voted	*vo-*

vot·ers	*vors*	war·ranted	*rM-*
voucher	*voCr*	war·ranty	*rMe*
		was	*3*
W		wash	*A*
		wash·ing	*A*
wage	*q*	wasn't	*zM*
wages	*js*	waste	*S*
wagon	*gn*	watch	*C*
wait	*a*	watch·ing	*C*
wait·ing	*a*	water	*lr*
waiver	*vr*	wa·ter·ing	*lr*
walk	*c*	wa·ters	*lrs*
wall	*l*	wa·ter·shed	*lrsd*
walls	*ls*	watt	*l*
wal·nut	*lnl*	wax	*x*
want	*M*	way	*a*
wanted	*M-*	ways	*as*
wants	*Ms*	we	*e*
war	*r*	we'd	*e'd*
ward	*w*	we'll	*e'l*
ware·house	*rhos*	we're	*e'r*
warn·ing	*rn*	we've	*e'v*
war·rant	*rM*	wear	*r*

wear·ing	_r_	west	_W_
weather	_ir_	west·erly	_Wrl_
weed	_d_	west·ern	_Wrn_
week	_c_	west·erner	_Wrnr_
week·end	_cn_	west·ward	_Ww_
weekly	_cl_	wet	_l_
weeks	_cs_	what	_l_
weigh	_a_	what's	_ls_
weigh·ing	_a_	what·ever	_lE_
weigh·ings	_a_	what·so·ever	_lsoE_
weight	_a_	wheat	_e_
weights	_as_	wheel	_l_
wel·come	_lk_	wheels	_ls_
wel·comed	_lk-_	when	_n_
wel·comes	_lks_	when·ever	_nE_
wel·com·ing	_lk_	where	_r_
welded	_ld-_	whereas	_rz_
weld·ing	_ld_	whereby	_rb_
wel·fare	_lfr_	wherein	_rn_
well	_l_	wher·ever	_rE_
wells	_ls_	whether	_lr_
went	_n_	which	_C_
were	_~_	which·ever	_CE_

while	*l*	will·ful	*lf*
white	*i*	will·fully	*lfl*
who	*hu*	will·ing	*l*
who·ever	*huE*	will·ingly	*ll*
whole	*hl*	will·ing·ness	*l'*
whole·heart·edly	*hlhrtl*	wills	*ls*
whole·sale	*hlsl*	win	*n*
wholly	*hll*	wind	*N*
whom	*h*	win·dow	*No*
whom·ever	*hE*	win·dows	*Nos*
whose	*hz*	wine	*n*
why	*y*	wing	*q*
wide	*d*	win·ner	*nr*
widely	*dl*	win·ners	*nrs*
wid·en·ing	*dn*	win·ter	*Nr*
wid·est	*dš*	wire	*r*
widow	*do*	wis·dom	*zd*
width	*dl*	wise	*z*
wife	*f*	wish	*4*
wil·der·ness	*ldŕ*	wished	*4-*
wild·life	*ldlf*	wishes	*4s*
will	*l*	wish·ing	*4*
willed	*l-*	wit	*i*

Word		Word	
with		won	
with·draw		won't	
with·drawal		won·der	
with·draw·als		won·der·ful	
with·draw·ing		won·der·ing	
with·drawn		wood	
with·draws		wood·lands	
with·drew		woods	
with·held		wool	
with·hold		word	
with·hold·ing		word·ing	
with·hold·ings		words	
with·holds		work	
within		work·book	
with·out		work·books	
with·stand		worked	
with·stand·ing		worker	
with·stands		work·ers	
with·stood		work·ing	
wit·ness		work·man	
wit·nesses		work·man·ship	
woman		work·men	
women		works	

work·shop	_osp_
world	_o_
worldly	_ol_
worlds	_os_
worn	_rn_
worse	_rs_
worth	_rt_
worth·while	_rtl_
wor·thy	_rte_
would	_d_
wouldn't	_dn_
write	_ri_
writer	_rir_
writ·ers	_rirs_
writ·ing	_ri_
writ·ten	_rtn_
wrong	_rq_
wrote	_ro_

X

x-ray	_ra_

Y

yard	yd
yards	yds
yard·stick	ydsc
year	yr
yearly	yrl
years	yrs
yel·low	ylo
yes	ys
yes·ter·day	ysrd
yes·ter·days	ysrds
yet	yt
yield	yld
you	u
you'd	u'd
you'll	u'l
you're	u'r
you've	u'v
young	yq
younger	ygr
young·sters	ygsrs
your	u

yours	*us*
your·self	*usf*
your·selves	*usvs*
youth	*ul*

Z

zero	*zro*
zip	*zp*
zone	*zn*
zones	*zns*
zon·ing	*zn‑*

INDEX OF BRIEF FORMS

ALPHABETICAL LISTING

a (an)	.	as (was)	*3*
able	*B*	associate	*aso*
about	*ab*	at (it)	*/*
accept	*ac*	be (been, but, buy, by)	*b*
accomplish	*ak*	been (be, but, buy, by)	*b*
acknowledge	*acy*	between	*bln*
administrate	*Am*	both	*bo*
advantage	*Avy*	business	*bs*
after	*af*	but (be, been, buy, by)	*b*
again (against)	*aq*	buy (be, been, but, by)	*b*
against (again)	*aq*	by (be, been, but, buy)	*b*
already	*Ar*	came (come, committee)	*k*
always	*a*	can	*c*
am (more)	⌒	character (characteristic)	*crc*
an (a)	.	characteristic (character)	*crc*
appreciate	*ap*	charge	*G*
appropriate	*apo*	circumstance	*Sk*
approximate	*apx*	come (came, committee)	*k*
are (our)	*r*	committee (came, come)	*k*
arrange	*ar*	complete	*kp*

congratulate	*kq*	firm	*fr*
consider	*ks*	for (full)	*f*
continue	*ku*	from	*f*
contract	*kc*	full (for)	*f*
contribute	*kb*	general	*jn*
control	*kl*	go (good)	*q*
convenience (convenient)	*kv*	good (go)	*q*
convenient (convenience)	*kv*	grate (great)	*gr*
correspond (correspondence)	*cor*	great (grate)	*gr*
correspondence (correspond)	*cor*	had (he, him)	*h*
customer	*K*	has	*hs*
deliver	*dl*	have (of, very)	*v*
determine	*dl*	he (had, him)	*h*
develop	*dv*	him (had, he)	*h*
difficult	*dfc*	his (is)	*)*
direct (doctor)	*dr*	hospital	*hsp*
distribute	*D*	immediate	*⌢*
doctor (direct)	*dr*	importance (important)	*pl*
during	*du*	important (importance)	*pl*
employ	*⌢p*	in (not)	*n*
ever (every)	*E*	include	*l*
every (ever)	*E*	individual	*nv*
experience	*vp*	industry	*n*

is (his)	)	own (on)	o
it (at)	/	part (port)	pt
letter	L	participate	pp
manage	~y	particular	ptc
manufacture	~y	perhaps	Ph
market	~r	please (up)	p
more (am)	~	point	py
necessary	nes	port (part)	pt
next	nx	present	p
not (in)	n	property	prp
note	nt	prove	pv
of (have, very)	v	public	pb
on (own)	o	refer	rf
once	oN	respond (response)	rsp
operate	op	response (respond)	rsp
opinion	opn	sample	sa
opportunity	opt	satisfactory (satisfy)	sat
order	od	satisfy (satisfactory)	sat
ordinary	ord	several	sv
organize	og	ship	A
other	ot	signature (significance, significant)	sig
our (are)	r		
over	O		

significance (signature, significant)	*sig*	up (please)	*p*
significant (signature, significance)	*sig*	us	*s*
situate	*sit*	usual	*uz*
specific (specify)	*sp*	very (have, of)	*v*
specify (specific)	*sp*	was (as)	*z*
standard	*sd*	we	*e*
success	*suc*	well (will)	*l*
suggest	*sug*	were (with)	*⌣*
that	*la*	why	*y*
the	*r*	will (well)	*l*
they	*ly*	with (were)	*⌣*
those	*loz*	work (world)	*⌣o*
to (too)	*l*	world (work)	*⌣o*
too (to)	*l*	would	*d*
under	*u*	your	*u*

INDEX OF ABBREVIATIONS

ALPHABETICAL LISTING

advertise	*av*	dollars (dollar)	*$*
agriculture	*agr*	east	*E*
America (American)	*a*	economic (economy)	*eco*
American (America)	*a*	economy (economic)	*eco*
amount	*amt*	enclose (enclosure)	*enc*
and	*+*	enclosure (enclose)	*enc*
attention	*all*	envelope	*env*
avenue	*ave*	especially	*esp*
billion	*B*	establish	*est*
boulevard	*blvd*	et cetera	*etc*
catalog	*cal*	example (executive)	*ex*
cent (cents)	*¢*	executive (example)	*ex*
cents (cent)	*¢*	federal	*fed*
Christmas	*Xmas*	feet	*ft*
company	*co*	government	*gvt*
corporation	*corp*	hour	*hr*
credit	*cr*	hundred	*H*
day	*d*	inch	*in*
department	*dpt*	incorporate (incorporated)	*inc*
dollar (dollars)	*$*	incorporated (incorporate)	*inc*

information	*inf*	question	*q*
insurance	*ins*	record	*rec*
invoice	*inv*	regard	*re*
junior	*jr*	represent (representative)	*rep*
literature	*lit*	representative (represent)	*rep*
merchandise	*mdse*	return	*ret*
million	*M*	second (secretary)	*sec*
Miss	*M*	secretary (second)	*sec*
month	*o*	senior	*sr*
Mr.	*r*	south	*S*
Mrs.	*rs*	square	*sq*
Ms.	*s*	street	*St*
north	*N*	superintendent	*S*
number	*No*	thousand	*T*
okay	*ok*	total	*tot*
ounce	*oz*	university	*U*
percent	*%*	vice president	*VP*
pound	*lb*	volume	*vol*
president	*P*	west	*W*
quart	*qt*	yard	*yd*

INDEX OF PHRASES

The following phrases are presented in alphabetical segments beginning with the pronouns I, we, and you plus a verb, followed by infinitive phrases (to plus a verb), high-frequency word combinations, and word combinations with words omitted.

The phrase list presents the 147 phrases in alphabetical segments.

Type	Number
"I" + a verb	25
"We" + a verb	26
"You" + a verb	20
"To" + a verb (infinitive phrase)	24
High-Frequency Word Combinations	44
Words Omitted and Word Compounds with a Word Omitted	8
Total	147

Phrase	Outline	Phrase	Outline
I am	‿	I know	*ino*
I appreciate	*iap*	I look	*ilc*
I believe	*iblv*	I shall	*isl*
I can	*ic*	I should	*isd*
I can be	*icb*	I was	
I cannot	*icn*	I will	
I could	*icd*	I will be	*ilb*
I do	*idu*	I would	*id*
I feel	*yfl*	I would appreciate	*idap*
I had	*ih*	I would be	*idb*
I have	*iv*	I would like	*idlc*
I have been	*ivb*	we appreciate	*eap*
I have had	*ivh*	we are	*er*
I hope	*ihp*	we are not	*ern*

we are pleased	*erp-*	you are	*ur*
we believe	*eblv*	you can	*uc*
we can	*ec*	you cannot	*ucn*
we can be	*ecb*	you can be	*ucb*
we cannot	*ecn*	you could	*ucd*
we could	*ecd*	you do	*udu*
we do	*edu*	you had	*uh*
we feel	*efl*	you have	*uv*
we had	*eh*	you have been	*uvb*
we have	*ev*	you have had	*uvh*
we have been	*evb*	you know	*uno*
we have had	*evh*	you need	*und*
we hope	*ehp*	you should	*usd*
we know	*eno*	you were	*u*
we shall	*esl*	you will	*ul*
we should	*esd*	you will be	*ulb*
we were	*e*	you will find	*ulfn*
we will	*el*	you would	*ud*
we will be	*elb*	you would be	*udb*
we would	*ed*	you would like	*udlc*
we would appreciate	*edap*	to be	*lb*
we would be	*edb*	to call	*lcl*
we would like	*edlc*	to come	*lk*

to determine	*(shorthand)*	as to	*(shorthand)*
to do	*(shorthand)*	as we	*(shorthand)*
to get	*(shorthand)*	as well as	*(shorthand)*
to give	*(shorthand)*	as you	*(shorthand)*
to go	*(shorthand)*	as your	*(shorthand)*
to have	*(shorthand)*	at the	*(shorthand)*
to have you	*(shorthand)*	can be	*(shorthand)*
to have your	*(shorthand)*	could be	*(shorthand)*
to hear	*(shorthand)*	fact that	*(shorthand)*
to keep	*(shorthand)*	for the	*(shorthand)*
to know	*(shorthand)*	for you	*(shorthand)*
to make	*(shorthand)*	for your	*(shorthand)*
to offer	*(shorthand)*	has been	*(shorthand)*
to pay	*(shorthand)*	have been	*(shorthand)*
to receive	*(shorthand)*	have had	*(shorthand)*
to say	*(shorthand)*	have not	*(shorthand)*
to see	*(shorthand)*	have you	*(shorthand)*
to send	*(shorthand)*	have your	*(shorthand)*
to use	*(shorthand)*	in the	*(shorthand)*
to visit	*(shorthand)*	it is	*(shorthand)*
to work	*(shorthand)*	of our	*(shorthand)*
and the	*(shorthand)*	of the	*(shorthand)*
as I	*(shorthand)*	of you	*(shorthand)*

of your	*vu*	will be	*lb*
on the	*σ*	will you	*lu*
on you	*ou*	will your	*lu*
on your	*ou*	would be	*db*
should be	*sdb*	would like	*dlc*
thank you	*lqu*	as soon as	*33*
that I	*lai*	nevertheless	*nvrls*
that we	*lae*	nonetheless	*nnls*
that you	*lau*	thank you for	*lqf*
that you are	*laur*	thank you for your	*lqf*
that you will	*laul*	thank you for your letter	*lqfL*
that your	*lau*	time to time	*LL*
to you	*lu*	up to date	*pda*
to your	*lu*		

IDENTIFICATION INITIALS FOR UNITED STATES AND TERRITORIES

Alabama (AL)	AL	Maryland (MD)	MD
Alaska (AK)	AK	Massachusetts (MA)	MA
Arizona (AZ)	AZ	Michigan (MI)	MI
Arkansas (AR)	AR	Minnesota (MN)	MN
California (CA)	CA	Mississippi (MS)	MS
Colorado (CO)	CO	Missouri (MO)	MO
Connecticut (CT)	CT	Montana (MT)	MT
Delaware (DE)	DE	Nebraska (NE)	NE
District of Columbia (DC)	DC	Nevada (NV)	NV
Florida (FL)	FL	New Hampshire (NH)	NH
Georgia (GA)	GA	New Jersey (NJ)	NJ
Hawaii (HI)	HI	New Mexico (NM)	NM
Idaho (ID)	ID	New York (NY)	NY
Illinois (IL)	IL	North Carolina (NC)	NC
Indiana (IN)	IN	North Dakota (ND)	ND
Iowa (IA)	IA	Ohio (OH)	OH
Kansas (KS)	KS	Oklahoma (OK)	OK
Kentucky (KY)	KY	Oregon (OR)	OR
Louisiana (LA)	LA	Pennsylvania (PA)	PA
Maine (ME)	ME	Rhode Island (RI)	RI

South Carolina (SC)	SC	West Virginia (WV)	WV
South Dakota (SD)	SD	Wisconsin (WI)	WI
Tennessee (TN)	TN	Wyoming (WY)	WY
Texas (TX)	TX		
Utah (UT)	UT	Canal Zone (CZ)	CZ
Vermont (VT)	VT	Guam (GU)	GU
Virginia (VA)	VA	Puerto Rico (PR)	PR
Washington (WA)	WA	Virgin Islands (VI)	VI

CANADIAN PROVINCES AND TERRITORIES

Alberta (AB)	*A B*	Nova Scotia (NS)	*NS*
British Columbia (BC)	*B C*	Ontario (ON)	*O N*
Manitoba (MB)	*M B*	Prince Edward Island (PE)	*P E*
New Brunswick (NB)	*N B*	Quebec (PQ)	*P Q*
Newfoundland (NF)	*N F*	Saskatchewan (SK)	*S K*
Northwest Territories (NT)	*N T*	Yukon Territory (YT)	*Y T*

METRIC TERMS

	(length) meter *m*	(capacity) liter *l*	(weight) gram *g*
kilo	km	kl	kg
hecto	hm	hl	hg
deca	dam	dal	dag
deci	dm	dl	dg
centi	cm	cl	cg
milli	mm	ml	mg
micro	crm	crl	crg
nano	nm	nl	ng

SUMMARY OF SPEEDWRITING SHORTHAND PRINCIPLES

BY ORDER OF PRESENTATION

1. Write what you hear — high — *hi*

2. Drop medial vowels — build — *bld*

3. Write initial and final vowels — office — *ofs* — fee — *fe*

4. Write **C** for the sound of *k* — copy — *cpe*

5. Write a capital **C** for the sound of *ch* — check — *Cc*

6. Write ⌒ for the sound of *m* — may — *⌒a*

7. Write ⌣ for the sound of *w* and *wh* — way — *⌣a* — when — *⌣n*

8. Underscore the last letter of any outline to add *ing* or *thing* as a word ending — billing — *bl̲* — something — *s⌒̲*

9. To form the plural of any outline ending in a mark of punctuation, double the last mark of punctuation — savings — *sv̲̲*

10. Write *ʂ* to form the plural of any outline, to show possession, or to add *ʂ* to a verb — books — *bcs* — runs — *rns*

11. Write *m* for the sounds of *mem* and *mum* — memo — *mo*

12. Write *m* for the sounds of *men, min, mon, mun* — menu — *mu* — money — *me*

13. Write *m* for the word endings
    mand, mend, mind, ment

    demand *dm*   amend *am*

    remind *rm*   payment *pam*

14. Write a capital *N* for the sound
    of *nt*

    sent *sN*

15. Write *sh* for the sound of *ish* or
    sh

    finish *fns*

16. Write a capital *A* for the word
    beginnings *ad, all, al*

    admit *ad*   also *Aso*

17. Write *m* for the initial sound of
    in or *en*

    indent *ndN*

18. Write *O* for the sound of *ow*

    allow *alo*

19. Write a printed capital *S*
    (joined) for the word beginnings *cer,
    cir, ser, sur*

    certain *Sln*   survey *Sva*

20. To form the past tense of a regular
    verb, write a hyphen after the outline

    used *u3-*

21. Write *l* for the sound of *ith* or
    th

    them *L*

22. Write *l* for the word ending *ly*
    or *ily*

    family *fl*

23. Write a capital *D* for the word
    beginning *dis*

    discuss *Dcs*

24. Write a capital *M* for the word
    beginning *mis*

    misplace *Mpls*

25. Retain beginning or ending vowels
    when building compound words

    payroll *parl*   headache *hdac*

26. Retain root-word vowels when adding
    prefixes and suffixes

    disappear *Dapr*   payment *pam*

27. Write a capital *P* (disjoined) for the word beginnings *per, pur, pre, pro, pro* (prah)

person   *Psn*   prepare   *Ppr*

provide   *Pvd*   problem   *Pbl*

28. Write *g* for the word ending *gram*

telegram   *Ulg*

29. Write *y* for the sound of *oi*

boy   *by*

30. For words ending in a long vowel + *t*, omit the *t* and write the vowel

rate   *ra*   meet   *⌒e*

31. Write *a* for the word beginning *an*

answer   *asr*

32. Write *g* for the medial or final sound of any vowel + *nk*

bank   *bg*   link   *lg*

33. Write a capital *S* (disjoined) for the word beginning *super* and for the word endings *scribe* and *script*

supervise   *Svz*   describe   *dS*

manuscript   *⌒mS*

34. Write *el* for the word beginning *electr*

electronic   *elnc*

35. Write *w* for the word ending *ward*

backward   *bcw*

36. Write *h* for the word ending *hood*

boyhood   *byh*

37. Write *∕* for the word ending *tion* or *sion*

vacation   *vcy*

38. Write *a* for the initial and final sound of *aw*

law   *la*   audit   *adl*

39. Write *g* for the sound of *kw*

quick   *qc*

40. Write a capital *N* for the sound of *nd*

friend   *frN*

41. Write *⌒* for the initial sound of *em* or *im*

emphasize   *⌒fsz*   impress   *⌒prs*

42. Omit *p* in the sound of *mpt* — prompt — *Pᴖⱡ*

43. Write *k* for the sounds of *com, con, coun, count* — common — *kn* — convey — *kva*

    counsel — *ksl* — account — *ak*

44. Write *ȣ* for the sound of *st* — rest — *rȣ*

45. Write *q* for the word ending *quire* — require — *rq*

46. Write *ȝ* for the sound of *zh* — pleasure — *plȝr*

47. Write *ʹ* for the word ending *ness* — kindness — *cNʹ*

48. Write ** for words beginning with the sound of any vowel + *x* — explain — *√pln* — accident — *√dN*

49. Write *∕x* for the medial and final sound of *x* — boxes — *bxȣ* — relax — *rlx*

50. Write *X* for the word beginnings *extr* and *extra* — extreme — *X⌐*

    extraordinary — *Xord*

51. Write *q* for the medial or final sound of any vowel + *ng* — rang — *rq* — single — *sgl*

52. Write *β* for the word endings *bil, ble, bly* — possible — *psβ* — probably — *Pbβ*

53. Omit the final *t* of a root word after the sound of *k* — act — *ac*

54. Write a slightly raised and disjoined *ι* for the word ending *ity* — quality — *qlᴵ*

55. Write *U* for the word beginning *un* — until — *ull*

56. Write *sl* for the sound of *shul* and for the word ending *chul* — financial — *fnnsl*

57. Write ⟨symbol⟩ for the sounds of *ance, ence, nce, nse* — expense ⟨outline⟩

58. Write ⟨symbol⟩ for the word beginning *sub* — submit ⟨outline⟩

59. Write ⟨symbol⟩ for the medial and final sound of *tive* — effective ⟨outline⟩

60. Write ⟨symbol⟩ for the word endings *ful* and *ify* — careful ⟨outline⟩   justify ⟨outline⟩

61. Write ⟨symbol⟩ for the word ending *ification* — qualifications ⟨outline⟩

62. Write a capital ⟨symbol⟩ for the word beginnings *enter, inter, intro* — enterprise ⟨outline⟩   introduce ⟨outline⟩   interest ⟨outline⟩

63. Write ⟨symbol⟩ for the word beginning and ending *self* — self-made ⟨outline⟩   myself ⟨outline⟩

64. Write ⟨symbol⟩ for the word ending *selves* — ourselves ⟨outline⟩

65. When a word contains two medial, consecutively pronounced vowels, write the first vowel — trial ⟨outline⟩

66. When a word ends in two consecutively pronounced vowels, write only the last vowel — idea ⟨outline⟩

67. Write ⟨symbol⟩ for the word beginnings *tran* and *trans* — transfer ⟨outline⟩